Penny Cook 1999

THE APPLE BARN
CIDER MILL & GENERAL STORE
Cookbook

VOLUME II

Johnathon

Granny Smith

Red Delicious

Golden Delicious

Rome Beauty

THE
APPL
Coo

*M*utsu

*F*uji

*G*ala

*W*inesap

BARN
book
VOLUME II

*J*onagold

The Apple Barn and Cider Mill
230 Apple Valley Road
Sevierville, Tennessee 37862
(423) 453-9319

ISBN: 0-9611508-3-1
Designed, manufactured, and edited by
Favorite Recipes Press
an imprint of

FRP™

2451 Atrium Way, Nashville, Tennessee 37214
1-800-358-0560

Cover Design: LaPrees Advertising & Design Services
Book Design: Bill Kersey
Project Manager: Ginger Ryan

Manufactured in the United States of America
First Printing: 1999 12,500 copies

Apple Variety images provided by Washington Apple Commission

Apple Varieties

Rome Beauty- Primarily used for cooking, this apple has a bright red color. Its most popular use is baked whole with a touch of brown sugar and honey.

Golden Delicious- A great all-purpose apple. Golden to light yellow-green in color with a rich, mellow flavor. Great for eating raw, but also retains its shape when baked or cooked.

Red Delicious- This apple is widely available year round and has a mild and sweet taste. It can be bright to dark red in color and is very juicy. Best used fresh in salads or to eat raw.

Granny Smith- A late season apple with a sharp, tart flavor. Green in color and usually associated with pies and other sweetened desserts.

Jonathan- This bright red apple is an older variety of apple with a moderately tart, distinctive flavor. It is good for both eating and baking.

Winesap- A slightly tart flavor and crisp texture makes this apple favorite of many. Deep red to violet red in color, it can be cooked and is also a favorite of our cider maker and wine master.

Mutsu (Crispin)- This green to yellow apple is best eaten raw. It is juicy and has a distinctive flavor that can be slightly tart. A cross between the Golden Delicious and Indo (a Japanese apple), it has similar cooking characteristics to the Golden Delicious.

Jonagold- A newer apple that is quickly becoming popular. It is a cross between a Golden Delicious and a Jonathan. It is a particularly good eating apple, with a very sweet and juicy taste.

Fuji- This apple has a orangish-yellow skin with a rosy blush. Its flesh is firm, crisp, and juicy. Excellent for eating raw.

Gala- A red skinned apple with firm and sweet white flesh. It is excellent for both eating raw and cooking.

Dedication

This cookbook is dedicated to

our loyal customers, whose

patronage, comments, and

suggestions have helped us to grow.

We would also like to thank

the wonderful folks at the

many farms and markets we

visited in the beginning of

our adventure. Their willingness

to share their experiences and

give advice has helped us create

The Apple Barn.

Contents

I must recount the beginnings of the Apple Barn to you second-hand, since I was not born yet when my parents Bill and Georgia Kilpatrick, along with Bon and Nancy Hicks purchased these rolling hills and fertile river bottom in 1971. They acquired the land which featured a farmhouse (which was rebuilt after being burned in 1921) and the original barn dating from the early 1900's from Roger Mullendore.

Bill and Georgia renovated and moved into the farmhouse in 1972. Dad was still a pharmacist in downtown Sevierville at that time. His pharmacy was on Bruce Street just across from Bon's business, Cash Hardware. The two had planned to eventually divide their recently purchased farm into a subdivision. But, at the time, it was on the outskirts of town, and it was decided to keep the property for a while. Mom and Dad both enjoyed the farm life, since they had themselves been raised on farms. I was born in 1974 and my brother, Kent, in 1979. So it seemed like the perfect place to raise their new family. Mr. Mullendore had a tobacco allotment for the farm, so a tobacco crop was maintained as well as about 60 head of beef cattle. I have fond memories of waking up early on winter mornings and "farming" with Dad. We would walk from the house to the barn (about 100 yards) and tend to the cattle. I would climb up into the hay loft and push the hay over into the feed rack. Mom was always worried that if Dad wasn't watching me close enough I would fall from the loft and the cattle and horses would eat me. After we were finished I would climb into the wheel barrow and Dad would ride me back to the house. He would then leave for a full day of dispensing medicine and Mom would take care of me, the house, and the farm during the day.

Then one year the tobacco crop was disease ridden. A University of Tennessee Agricultural Consultant came to investigate and advise when he noticed some fruit trees in our yard. Dad had planted these as a hobby (as evidenced by his extensive library of horticultural and fruit tree books from the 1970's). The consultant along with our county agent noted that the trees were flourishing and conducted soil tests which confirmed that we had a good location for growing apples. This is where the legend really begins.

In the winter of 1976-1977 we planted 1100 trees in four varieties: Golden Delicious, Red Delicious, Rome Beauty, and Jonathan. Dad remembers that it took longer than it should have to plant the trees because every time they had a hole ready to plant the tree, I would jump in it and play in the dirt (I was 3 years old at the time). We continued to plant more trees in the subsequent years. They flourished and our first decent crops of apples came in 1980 and 1981. With Dad at the drugstore during the day, Mom and I would bag a few of the apples and sell them out of our carport at the house.

In 1981 Bon and my Dad took the big step of converting the hay and cattle barn into the Apple Barn. Every board of the barn was pressure washed and it was literally scrubbed from top to bottom. We opened for business in the fall of 1981 offering only apples and cider. We were open for only two months. Irvin Pitts, an architect friend of Dad's, who was instrumental in the early planning process, advised us on some structural modifications. Two of the original stables were converted to cold storage for cider and apples. Other stables were floored with locally sawed white pine and converted into display areas for jams, jellies, apple butter, molasses, smoked country ham, bacon, dried fruits, and nuts.

Customers were soon demanding a place to enjoy a cup of fresh cider, along with some snacks. So, in 1982 we added the Cider Bar to the rear of the barn, with an outside deck extending into the orchard. Its center piece is an antique soda fountain and back bar from my grandfather, William Kilpatrick's drugstore in Vonore, Tennessee. It is a beautiful focal point made of cherry, onyx, and Tennessee pink marble. Dad says he can remember standing on a milk crate to scoop into deep ice cream tubs when he was young. Apple Barn guests enjoy hot or cold cider, apple dumplings, fried apple pies, fresh baked apple pies, and other apple goodies still served today over this historical soda fountain.

The Apple Barn continued to grow in the following years, adding more products, gaining more customers, and staying open a little longer. Nancy Hicks, Bon's wife, worked during this time crafting arrangements, wreaths, and indian corn arrangements to give our customers more to browse through than just apples. As we grew, it became evident that Pat Kent, who was cooking our delicacies for the cider bar and making apple butter for sale in the barn, would need an on site kitchen. So, in 1983 we completed the Apple Pie Kitchen (which has since been renovated and expanded twice). Pat and her staff continue to this day to fry pies, cook apple butter, and cook an assortment of our now famous Apple Barn products. Pat says on busy days in the fall they make as many as 5,000 fried pies a day- all still done by hand!

Customers loved coming to the farm for our pies and cider, but quickly began asking if we had a place where they could sit down and enjoy a full meal. Dad and Bon discussed the fact that they had no restaurant operation experience, so they decided to bring in a partner who had operated some other successful restaurants in the area. In 1986 the decision was made to convert our home, the original 1921 farmhouse, to the Applewood Farmhouse Restaurant. It opened in 1987 and has been a success from the very beginning. It was also in 1987 that we built the Candy Apple and Chocolate Factory (which was renovated and expanded in 1997). It features caramel and candied apples, apple-walnut fudge, old-fashioned stick candy, and other treats, all of which are made right here behind large windows for our customers to watch. It was also in 1986-1987 that Dad left the pharmacy to manage the farm full-time. I think he has had a smile on his face ever since.

In 1988 we completed a major renovation of the barn itself. That old hay loft that I used to feed the livestock from is now open to the public. We display local crafts and gift items there and added a third level exclusively for baskets. With the help of our ice cream expert, David Frangella, we opened the Creamery in 1991. David makes several flavors of homemade ice cream, as well as old fashioned shakes, malts, and sundaes. With the continuing success of all the establishments, we decided to build the Apple Barn Winery in 1994. The winery is one of the most advanced in the state, and a leading producer of fruit wines. Some favorites are: Apple Blush, Apple-Raspberry, Apple-Strawberry, and Orchard White. The wines have received several medals from wine competitions and conventions from around the country.

The original restaurant was bursting at the seams with as much as a two hour waiting line for a table during the busy season. So, our partners suggested a second, very similar restaurant on the farm. The Applewood Farmhouse Grill opened in 1995 with a slightly lighter menu than the original with more sandwiches and ala carte items than the original.

As you can see, our love of apples has led to a lot of growth here in "Apple Valley." Through the support of Bon and Nancy, the vision and hard work of Mom and Dad, and our "family" of employees, we have become a real destination for folks visiting East Tennessee and the beautiful Great Smoky Mountains National Park. This cookbook, our second, attempts to capture the magic of apples and the spirit of the Apple Barn Cider Mill and General Store. Whether you are a regular visitor, or have never been to our farm, I invite you to come visit us.

Kevin William Kilpatrick

Appetizers & Salads

Hillsides covered with trees in various stages of apple production surround the Apple Barn, dedicated to the celebration of this historic fruit.

Apple Bisque

1 (25-ounce) jar Apple Barn™ applesauce
1 (28-ounce) jar Apple Barn™ apple butter
1 cup apple juice
4 cups half-and-half
1 teaspoon cinnamon
1/2 teaspoon ground cloves
1/2 teaspoon allspice

Combine applesauce, apple butter, apple juice, half-and-half, cinnamon, cloves and allspice in large bowl and mix well. Chill, covered, until serving time. Ladle into soup bowls. Garnish with lemon slices and mint sprigs.

Yield: 20 servings

Fifty-six different kinds of apples were served at a banquet given by the Grand Duke Cosmo III of Tuscany in 1670.

Apple Soup

1½ cups chopped cooked chicken
4 cups chicken broth
1 onion, sliced
3 tomatoes, peeled, chopped, or 1 can
   chopped tomatoes
1 carrot, sliced
1 rib celery, sliced
1 red bell pepper, sliced
3 tart apples, peeled, sliced
3 tablespoons butter
2 tablespoons all-purpose flour
1 teaspoon dry mustard
2 teaspoons curry powder
Salt and pepper to taste

Combine chicken and 3 cups of broth in Dutch oven. Cook until heated through. Sauté onion, tomatoes, carrot, celery, red pepper and apples in butter in skillet until tender. Sprinkle with flour and stir until blended. Pour 1 cup of broth over vegetables and stir until well blended. Stir vegetables into chicken and broth. Simmer, partially covered, for 10 minutes. Add mustard and curry powder. Simmer, partially covered, for 15 minutes. Season with salt and pepper.

Yield: 6 servings

Swedish Dessert Soup

4 cups apple juice
¼ cup tapioca
1 lemon, thinly sliced
6 whole cloves
¼ teaspoon nutmeg
1 (11-ounce) can mandarin oranges, drained
1 (16-ounce) can pineapple chunks, drained
1 (10-ounce) package frozen strawberries in
   syrup, thawed
⅓ cup grenadine syrup
⅛ teaspoon salt

Bring apple juice, tapioca, lemon, cloves and nutmeg to boil in saucepan. Simmer for 10 minutes, stirring frequently. Combine oranges, pineapple, strawberries, grenadine syrup and salt in large bowl and mix gently. Add apple juice mixure to fruit mixture. Chill until serving time. Garnish servings with whipped cream or sour cream. May substitute cranberry juice cocktail for apple juice if preferred.

Yield: 6 servings

If you would like to freeze cider, pour about 1 cup of cider from each gallon to allow for expansion during freezing. Do not serve cider until all ice is melted. To thaw cider, leave at room temperature or in the refrigerator until completely thawed. This process can be expedited by submersing in hot water or by defrosting in microwave. Shake well before serving.

Three Alarm Fire

1 (12-ounce) jar pineapple preserves
1 (10-ounce) jar Apple Barn™ apple jelly
½ (8-ounce) jar prepared horseradish
1 tablespoon dry mustard
8 ounces cream cheese

Mix pineapple preserves, apple jelly, horseradish and dry mustard in bowl. Pour over cream cheese on serving plate. Serve with wheat or bran crackers.

Yield: 12 to 18 servings

Piña Colada Fruit Dip

1 (3-ounce) package coconut instant
   pudding mix
3/4 cup milk
1 (8-ounce) can crushed pineapple
1/2 cup yogurt

Combine pudding mix, milk, pineapple
and yogurt in blender container. Process for
30 seconds, stirring once. Refrigerate for
several hours. Serve with fresh cherries,
melon, apples or pears.

Yield: 2¹/₂ cups

Fudge Sauce for Fruit

1 cup margarine
2 (14-ounce) cans sweetened condensed
   milk
12 ounces chocolate chips

Combine margarine, condensed milk
and chocolate chips in saucepan. Cook
over low heat until chocolate melts, stirring
frequently. Serve with sliced apples, pears,
bananas and strawberries.

Yield: 4 cups

Roquefort Cheese Ball

8 ounces Roquefort cheese, softened
16 ounces cream cheese, softened
3 tablespoons margarine, softened
½ cup chopped black olives
½ cup chopped parsley

Combine Roquefort cheese, cream cheese and margarine in mixer bowl and mix until smooth. Add black olives and mix well. Chill in refrigerator. Shape into ball and coat with parsley. Place on serving plate. Serve with crackers or apple slices. May substitute pecans for parsley.

Yield: 12 servings

Waldorf Tea Sandwiches

2 cups peeled grated Golden Delicious
   apples
½ cup finely chopped celery
⅔ cup finely chopped English walnuts
1 cup (or more) mayonnaise
20 thin slices cinnamon-raisin bread, crusts
   removed

Combine apples, celery and walnuts in bowl and mix well. Add enough mayonnaise to make of spreading consistency. Spread over ½ bread slices. Top with remaining bread slices. Cut each sandwich into 4 rectangles or squares.

Yield: 40 servings

*Make a delicious Waldorf Salad out of chopped unpeeled apples, raisins,
walnuts and mayonnaise. Use your own proportions
to customize the salad.*

Apple Salad

3 to 4 tablespoons whipped topping
2 tablespoons mayonnaise
$\frac{1}{2}$ (3-ounce) package lemon or lime gelatin
6 or 7 apples, chopped
1 cup chopped nuts
Salt to taste

Combine whipped topping and mayonnaise in bowl and mix well. Sprinkle gelatin over whipped topping and mix well. Toss apples and nuts in whipped topping mixture. Add salt and mix well. Chill, covered, until serving time.

Yield: 6 to 8 servings

Make a special Yogurt Salad Dressing by substituting lemon or vanilla yogurt for all or part of the mayonnaise in Waldorf salad or fruited coleslaw.

Almond Apple Salad

¼ cup vegetable oil
2 tablespoons sugar
2 tablespoons malt vinegar
¼ teaspoon salt
⅛ teaspoon almond extract
6 cups torn mixed greens
3 medium apples, cut into wedges
1 cup thinly sliced celery
2 tablespoons sliced green onions
⅓ cup slivered almonds

Combine oil, sugar, vinegar, salt and almond extract in jar with tightfitting lid. Shake to mix well. Refrigerate for several hours. Combine mixed greens, apples, celery, green onions and almonds in bowl. Pour salad dressing over salad and toss gently to coat. Serve immediately.

Yield: 8 servings

Autumn Fruit Salad

1 cup vanilla yogurt
1 teaspoon cinnamon
1/4 teaspoon ginger
1/2 teaspoon nutmeg
1 tablespoon apple cider
2 Red Delicious apples, cut into 1-inch chunks
1 Granny Smith apple, cut into 1-inch chunks
1 banana, sliced into 1/2-inch rounds
2 Bartlett pears, cut into 1-inch chunks
1/2 pound red grapes, halved
1/2 cup toasted almond slivers

Combine yogurt, cinnamon, ginger, nutmeg and apple cider in bowl and mix well. Combine apples, banana, pears, grapes and almonds in large bowl. Pour yogurt mixture over fruit mixture. Toss to coat. Chill until ready to serve. May peel apples and pears if desired.

Yield: 8 servings

Cinnamon Apple Salad

½ cup red hot cinnamon candies
2 cups water
1 (3-ounce) package lemon gelatin
2 tablespoons lemon juice
1¼ cups chopped apples
¼ cup chopped walnuts
13 ounces cream cheese, softened
¼ cup heavy cream
⅛ teaspoon salt

Combine cinnamon candies and water in saucepan. Cook for 5 minutes or until candies dissolve, stirring frequently. Add gelatin and stir until dissolved. Cool to room temperature. Add lemon juice. Chill until partially set. Fold in apples and walnuts. Spoon ½ of mixture into 8x8-inch dish. Chill until set. Combine cream cheese, cream and salt in bowl and mix well. Spoon evenly over congealed layer. Spread remaining gelatin mixture carefully over top. Chill until set. Cut into squares and serve on salad greens.

Yield: 8 servings

Cranberry Apple Salad

2 (16-ounce) cans whole cranberry sauce
2 cups boiling water
2 (3-ounce) packages raspberry gelatin
2 tablespoons lemon juice
1/2 teaspoon salt
1 cup mayonnaise
2 cups chopped apples
1/2 cup chopped nuts

Melt cranberry sauce in saucepan over medium heat. Drain, reserving juice, and set aside. Combine juice, water and gelatin in bowl and stir until gelatin is dissolved. Add lemon juice and salt. Chill, covered, in refrigerator until mixture mounds on spoon. Add mayonnaise and beat until smooth. Fold in cranberries, apples and nuts. Pour into 2-quart mold. Chill in refrigerator for several hours or until set.

Yield: 10 to 12 servings

Fresh Apple Salad

1 (20-ounce) can pineapple chunks
¼ cup butter or margarine
¼ cup sugar
1 tablespoon lemon juice
1 tablespoon cornstarch
2 tablespoons water
1 cup mayonnaise
2 cups seedless grapes
8 cups chopped Red Delicious apples
1 to 2 teaspoons poppy seeds
1½ cups toasted pecans

Drain pineapple, reserving juice. Combine reserved pineapple juice, butter, sugar and lemon juice in saucepan and heat to boiling. Mix cornstarch and water in small bowl and stir into hot mixture. Let cool completely. Stir in mayonnaise. Combine pineapple, grapes, apples and poppy seeds in large bowl. Add dressing and mix well. Chill. Stir in pecans just before serving.

Yield: 16 servings

Green Apple and Salmon Salad

3 Granny Smith apples, finely chopped
1 (14-ounce) can pink salmon, drained
¾ cup chopped walnuts
1 to 2 tablespoons mayonnaise-type
    salad dressing

Combine apples and salmon in large bowl. Add walnuts and mix well. Add enough salad dressing to bind mixture. Chill, covered, overnight.

Yield: 6 servings

Kiwi Apple Salad

3 large apples, chopped
2 kiwi, chopped
2 cups sliced seedless grapes
1 cup miniature marshmallows
½ cup raisins (optional)
8 ounces whipped topping

Combine apples, kiwi, grapes, marshmallows, raisins and whipped topping in bowl and mix well. Serve on lettuce leaves.

Yield: 8 to 10 servings

Minted Fruit Salad

1 (16-ounce) can unsweetened pineapple
   chunks
1 banana, sliced
1 Red Delicious apple, chopped
1 green apple, chopped
1 pear, chopped
1/2 cup orange juice
2 tablespoons chopped fresh mint
1 tablespoon honey

Drain pineapple, reserving juice. Combine banana, apples and pear in serving dish. Mix reserved pineapple juice, orange juice, mint and honey in bowl. Pour over fruit. Chill, covered, for 3 1/2 hours, stirring occasionally.

Yield: 4 to 6 servings

*John Chapman is one American folk hero who was a real person. Beginning
in 1806 he loaded two canoes with bags of apple seeds and traveled
down the Ohio River, stopping to set out orchards in the wilderness along the way.
For forty years he traveled through Ohio, Indiana and Illinois, caring
for his orchards. Before his death he had accumulated 1200 acres of apple orchards.
The state of Ohio observes "Johnny Appleseed Day," and four
monuments stand in his memory.*

29

Stuffed Apple Salad

4 ribs celery hearts, finely chopped
6 Red Delicious apples
2 tablespoons lemon juice
1 cup whipping cream
4 teaspoons lemon juice
2 tablespoons raw sugar
½ clove of garlic, finely chopped
1 teaspoon white pepper
⅛ teaspoon salt
½ cup golden raisins
2 tablespoons pine nuts
½ cup chopped walnuts

Combine celery with ice water to cover in bowl. Let stand until crisp. Drain and pat dry. Wipe apples with damp cloth to polish. Cut ½-inch slice off top. Scoop out pulp and seeds carefully, leaving shell. Discard seeds. Chop pulp finely. Combine pulp and 2 tablespoons lemon juice in bowl and mix well. Stir in celery. Beat whipping cream in mixer bowl until soft peaks form. Fold in 4 teaspoons lemon juice, sugar, garlic, white pepper, salt, raisins, pine nuts and walnuts. Pour whipped cream mixture over apple mixture, tossing to coat. Spoon into apple shells. Garnish with walnut halves or drained whole maraschino cherries with stems. Serve on bed of watercress or lettuce. Serve with small wedges of cheese.

Yield: 6 servings

Toffee Apple Salad

1 (8-ounce) can crushed pineapple
1 tablespoon all-purpose flour
½ cup sugar
2 tablespoons apple cider vinegar
1 egg, beaten
4 cups chopped apples
8 ounces whipped topping
2 cups salted Spanish peanuts, chopped

Drain pineapple, reserving juice. Combine reserved pineapple juice, flour, sugar, vinegar and egg in small saucepan. Cook until thickened, stirring constantly. Cool. Combine apples, pineapple, whipped topping and pineapple juice mixture in 2½-quart bowl and mix well. Chill until serving time. Stir in peanuts just before serving.

Yield: 8 servings

Susan's Tossed Apple Salad

Salad

1 head Romaine lettuce, torn into bite-size
   pieces
2 or 3 Red Delicious apples, sliced, tossed in
   apple cider or lemon juice
1 pound sharp Cheddar cheese, cubed
Dijon Mustard Dressing
1 cup roasted pecan halves

Combine lettuce, apples and cheese in large bowl. Pour Dijon Mustard Dressing over salad. Add pecans and toss lightly.

Dijon Mustard Dressing

1 1/2 tablespoons cider vinegar
1 tablespoon grainy Dijon mustard
1 tablespoon fresh chives
4 1/2 tablespoons corn oil
3 tablespoons heavy cream
Salt and pepper to taste

Whisk vinegar, Dijon mustard, chives, corn oil and cream in bowl. Season with salt and pepper.

Yield: 4 to 6 servings

Dried Cherry Chicken Salad

4 chicken breast halves, cooked, chopped
1 cup dried red tart cherries
3 ribs celery, coarsely chopped
2 Granny Smith apples, coarsely chopped
1 cup coarsely chopped pecans
1¼ cups mayonnaise
½ cup chopped parsley
1 tablespoon raspberry vinegar
Salt and pepper to taste

Combine chicken, cherries, celery, apples and pecans in large bowl. Mix mayonnaise, parsley and vinegar in medium bowl. Stir into chicken mixture and toss to coat. Season with salt and pepper. Chill for 2 hours or longer. Serve on bed of red leaf lettuce. Garnish with additional cherries.

Yield: 6 servings

The apple tree is a member of the rose family. The blossoms are less fragrant than rose blossoms, but an apple is a more delicious fruit than the rose hip.

Curried Chicken and Rice Salad

4 chicken breast halves, cooked, chopped
1 package wild rice, cooked
1 cup seedless green grapes
1 cup chopped celery
1 cup slivered almonds
1 cup chopped apples
1/2 cup mayonnaise
1 tablespoon mango chutney
2 tablespoons soy sauce
2 to 3 teaspoons curry powder

Mix chicken, rice, grapes, celery, almonds and apples in bowl. Add mayonnaise and mix well. Add chutney, soy sauce and curry powder and mix well. Adjust seasonings if necessary. Chill for 2 hours.

Yield: 4 to 6 servings

Fruit and Chicken Salad

16 ounces chicken breast strips
1/2 cup plain low-fat yogurt
1/4 cup reduced-fat mayonnaise
1/4 teaspoon cinnamon
3/4 cup unsweetened apple juice
3/4 cup water
2 cups long grain and wild rice
3/4 cup chopped MacIntosh apple
1/2 cup sliced celery
1/2 cup chopped pecans
25 to 30 small seedless red grapes

Rinse chicken and pat dry. Combine yogurt, mayonnaise and cinnamon in small bowl. Cover and chill. Combine chicken, apple juice and water in saucepan. Simmer, covered, over medium heat for 15 to 20 minutes or until chicken is cooked through. Remove chicken from pan and reserve pan juices. Chop chicken. Place in bowl. Cover and chill. Cook rice according to package directions, using reserved pan juices and adding enough water to equal amount of liquid needed. Toss rice, apple, celery, pecans and grapes together gently in bowl. Stir in chicken and yogurt mixture. Chill until serving time. Garnish with spinach leaves or fresh fruit slices.

Yield: 6 servings

Honey Mustard Turkey Salad

½ cup fat-free mayonnaise
2 tablespoons honey
1½ tablespoons Dijon mustard
¾ teaspoon lite soy sauce
¾ teaspoon lemon juice
2 cups chopped cooked turkey
¼ cup chopped green onions
½ cup chopped celery
2 small or 1 large apple, chopped
¼ green bell pepper, chopped
¼ cup toasted almonds or cashews
½ cup raisins, or 1 cup seedless red grapes

Mix mayonnaise, honey, Dijon mustard, soy sauce and lemon juice in small bowl. Combine turkey, green onions, celery, apple, green pepper, almonds and raisins in large bowl. Add honey mustard sauce and mix well. Chill for 2 hours. Serve on lettuce leaves. Garnish with nuts or chow mein noodles.

Yield: 4 to 6 servings

Tuna Stuffed Apple Stars

4 medium apples, cored
1/2 bunch leaf lettuce, separated
2 tablespoons lemon juice
1 (7-ounce) can water-pack tuna, drained
2 hard-boiled eggs, chopped
1/4 cup chopped sweet pickle
1/4 cup finely chopped onion
2 tablespoons finely chopped pimento
1/4 teaspoon salt
Pepper to taste
1/3 cup mayonnaise

Arrange apples on lettuce-lined platter. Cut each into 6 wedges, cutting to but not through bottom; spread wedges apart. Brush cut surfaces with 1 tablespoon lemon juice to prevent browning. Break tuna into chunks in bowl and sprinkle with remaining lemon juice. Stir in eggs, sweet pickle, onion, pimento, salt, pepper and mayonnaise. Spoon into apples. Garnish with carrot curls. Serve immediately.

Yield: 4 servings

Old-Fashioned Pineapple Dressing

3/4 cup sugar
2 teaspoons cornstarch
1/4 cup lemon juice
5 tablespoons orange juice
1 cup pineapple juice
2 eggs, beaten
2 tablespoons butter
4 ounces whipped cream

Combine sugar and cornstarch in saucepan and mix well. Stir in lemon juice, orange juice, pineapple juice and eggs. Add butter. Cook over medium heat until thickened, stirring constantly. Cool. Stir in whipped cream. Serve as dressing for sliced apples. May be stored in refrigerator for several days.

Yield: 2 to 3 cups

Entrées, Sides
and Breads

It's not necessary to live in Sevierville to enjoy the delights of the Apple Barn. Our products, from applewood smoked ham to homemade candy and jellies, are shipped world-wide.

Apple Chicken

2½ pounds chicken pieces
½ teaspoon salt
¼ teaspoon pepper
2 to 3 tablespoons corn oil
1 (21-ounce) can Apple Barn™ apple
    pie filling
½ cup dry white wine
½ cup orange juice
¼ cup packed light brown sugar
½ teaspoon salt
¼ teaspoon allspice
¼ teaspoon nutmeg
¼ teaspoon ground cloves

Season chicken with ½ teaspoon salt and pepper. Cook chicken in corn oil in large skillet over medium-high heat for 10 minutes on each side; drain. Combine pie filling, wine, orange juice, brown sugar, ½ teaspoon salt, allspice, nutmeg and cloves in bowl and mix well. Pour over chicken. Simmer, covered, for 20 to 25 minutes or until chicken is tender. Serve with rice.

Yield: 4 servings

Apple-Glazed Chicken

16 ounces boneless skinless chicken breasts
1/3 cup Apple Barn™ apple jelly
2 tablespoons dry sherry
2 teaspoons lemon juice
1/4 teaspoon salt
3/4 cup seedless red grape halves
3 sprigs of parsley, chopped

Rinse chicken and pat dry. Heat skillet sprayed with nonstick cooking spray over medium-high heat. Add chicken. Cook for 8 to 10 minutes or until cooked through, turning once. Remove to serving platter. Mix jelly, wine, lemon juice and salt in bowl. Add to skillet. Cook until jelly melts, stirring constantly. Stir in grapes and parsley. Cook until heated through. Spoon over chicken.

Yield: 4 servings

Make a delicious Apple Stuffing with equal parts chopped apples and bread cubes. Season with onion, celery, sage and salt.

Apple-Stuffed Chicken Breasts

4 whole chicken breasts, boned,
   skinned, split
1 small onion, finely chopped
1 clove of garlic, crushed
2 tablespoons margarine
1 apple, peeled, shredded
¾ cup soft bread crumbs
½ teaspoon salt
¼ teaspoon rosemary
½ teaspoon basil
All-purpose flour
2 tablespoons margarine
¾ cup apple juice
2 tablespoons brandy
½ cup whipping cream
Pepper to taste

Rinse chicken and pat dry. Place between layers of plastic wrap. Pound to ¼-inch thickness. Sauté onion and garlic in 2 tablespoons margarine in large saucepan until tender. Stir in apple, bread crumbs, salt, rosemary and basil and mix well. Cook over low heat until heated through, stirring constantly. Spoon small amount of apple mixture onto boned side of each chicken breast half. Roll to enclose filling, tucking in ends; secure with wooden picks. Coat chicken with flour. Brown on all sides in 2 tablespoons margarine in large skillet. Remove to plate. Add apple juice and brandy to skillet; mix well. Add chicken. Simmer, covered, for 25 to 30 minutes or until tender, turning once. Remove chicken to plate. Cover chicken and keep warm in oven. Add cream to pan drippings in skillet and mix well. Bring to boil, stirring constantly. Simmer until sauce is reduced and slightly thickened, stirring frequently. Add pepper and mix well. Remove and discard wooden picks from chicken. Arrange chicken on serving platter. Top with cream sauce.

Yield: 8 servings

43

Dixie Pork Chops

8 pork chops
3 tablespoons shortening
$\frac{1}{2}$ teaspoon salt
Pepper to taste
4 apples, sliced into rings
$\frac{1}{2}$ cup packed brown sugar
2 tablespoons all-purpose flour
1 cup water
Several drops of vinegar
$\frac{1}{2}$ teaspoon sage
$\frac{1}{2}$ cup seedless raisins

Brown pork chops in shortening in skillet. Remove pork chops to baking dish, reserving pan drippings. Sprinkle pork chops with salt and pepper. Top with apples; sprinkle with brown sugar. Stir flour, water, vinegar and sage into reserved pan drippings in skillet. Cook until thickened, stirring constantly. Stir in raisins. Pour over pork chops. Bake at 350 degrees for 1 hour.

Yield: 8 servings

Fall Pork Chops

6 (½-inch) pork chops
1½ cups apple cider or apple juice
1 tablespoon sugar
¼ teaspoon curry powder
1 teaspoon salt
6 pitted prunes
12 dried apricot halves
2 tablespoons cornstarch
2 tablespoons water

Brown pork chops on both sides in preheated 325-degree electric skillet. Combine apple cider, sugar, curry powder and salt in bowl; mix well. Pour over pork chops. Arrange prunes and apricots over pork chops. Simmer, covered, for 1 hour or until done to taste. Remove pork chops and fruit to serving platter. Stir mixture of cornstarch and water into pan drippings. Cook until thickened, stirring constantly. Pour over pork chops.

Yield: 6 servings

Mix warm or chilled applesauce with a generous amount of horseradish for a delicious Applesauce Horseradish Accompaniment for beef or pork.

Pork Chops and Apples in Mustard Sauce

2 pounds apples, peeled, thinly sliced
4 (³/₄-inch-thick) pork loin chops
Salt to taste
1 tablespoon butter or margarine
¹/₄ cup dry white wine
1 cup whipping cream
¹/₃ cup Dijon mustard
Pepper to taste

Arrange apples in lightly greased 9x9-inch baking dish. Bake at 400 degrees for 15 minutes. Sprinkle pork chops with salt. Brown in butter in skillet over medium heat for 7 to 8 minutes on each side. Arrange on top of apples. Add wine to skillet. Cook until liquid is reduced by half, stirring to deglaze skillet. Pour over pork chops. Combine cream and Dijon mustard in small bowl. Season with salt and pepper. Pour over pork chops, shaking dish to distribute cream around apples. Bake at 400 degrees for 15 minutes or until pork chops are cooked through.

Yield: 4 servings

Roast Pork with Apples

1 (5-pound) pork loin roast with ribs
1 teaspoon sage
4 teaspoons salt
½ teaspoon pepper
1 medium apple
½ cup Apple Barn™ apple jelly, melted

Cut between ribs of roast about ¾ of way through. Rub mixture of sage, salt and pepper into roast, including slits. Place fat side up on rack in shallow pan. Roast at 325 degrees for 2½ hours or to 175 degrees on meat thermometer. Cut apple into ½-inch rings; cut rings into halves. Insert peeling side up into slits in roast. Brush generously with jelly. Bake for 30 minutes longer or to 180 degrees on meat thermometer, basting frequently with remaining jelly. Let stand for 30 minutes.

Yield: 8 servings

Add grated apple to mint relish for a refreshing accompaniment to beef or lamb.

Ham Apple Pie

2¼ cups all-purpose flour
½ teaspoon baking powder
½ teaspoon salt
½ cup butter
1 cup whipping cream
¼ cup sugar or honey
1 tablespoon all-purpose flour
Salt to taste
½ teaspoon cinnamon
1 cup raisins
5 tart apples, peeled, sliced
1 pound deli-style ham, sliced
2 tablespoons butter
1 egg, beaten
2 tablespoons milk

Combine 2¼ cups flour, baking powder and ½ teaspoon salt in bowl; mix well. Cut in ½ cup butter until crumbly. Blend in whipping cream. Chill, wrapped in plastic wrap, for 30 minutes or until firm. Roll ¼ inch thick on lightly floured surface. Trim to 14-inch length. Place on greased and floured baking sheet. Cut trimmings into strips. Combine sugar, 1 tablespoon flour, salt to taste, cinnamon and raisins in bowl; mix well. Add apples. Toss to coat. Arrange ham slices over pastry. Spread apple mixture over ham to within 2 inches of edge of pastry. Dot with 2 tablespoons butter. Fold edges over filling; pinch corners. Arrange pastry strips lattice-fashion on top. Brush with mixture of egg and milk. Bake at 375 degrees for 30 to 40 minutes or until golden brown.

Yield: 4 to 6 servings

Apple Beef Stroganoff

3 cups apple juice
1 envelope brown gravy mix
1 envelope onion soup mix
2 teaspoons beef bouillon
1 pound stew beef, cut into bite-size pieces
Slivered carrots to taste

Combine apple juice, gravy mix, soup mix and bouillon in Dutch oven and mix well. Add beef and carrots. Bake, covered, at 325 degrees for 3 hours or until beef is tender. Serve with boiled small potatoes or buttered egg noodles.

Yield: 4 to 6 servings

Make a delicious Ham Sauce by stirring 1/4 cup each apple juice and raisins into ham drippings in skillet. Simmer for 2 minutes and add 1/2 cup chunky applesauce. Cook until heated through.

Applesauce Meatballs

1 egg
1/2 cup milk
1 1/2 cups croutons
1 1/2 pounds lean ground beef
2/3 cup Apple Barn™ applesauce
3 tablespoons chopped onion
1/2 teaspoon salt
1/8 teaspoon pepper
1 (10-ounce) can tomato soup
1/2 soup can water

Beat egg and milk in bowl until smooth. Add croutons and mix well. Let stand for 5 minutes. Beat until light and fluffy. Add ground beef, applesauce, onion, salt and pepper and mix well. Shape into meatballs. Place in 9x13-inch baking dish. Pour mixture of soup and water over top. Bake at 350 degrees for 45 minutes. Serve with buttered noodles.

Yield: 6 servings

Apple Meat Loaf

3 eggs
3 tablespoons prepared horseradish
2 teaspoons salt
2 tablespoons prepared mustard
¾ cup ketchup
1 large onion, minced
1½ cups bread crumbs
2 cups peeled, finely chopped apples
2½ pounds lean ground beef

Combine eggs, horseradish, salt, mustard and ketchup in large bowl and mix well. Stir in onion, bread crumbs and apples. Add ground beef and mix well. Shape into loaf and place in greased 5x9-inch loaf pan. Bake at 350 degrees for 1 hour and 15 minutes or until cooked through.

Yield: 8 to 10 servings

51

Apple Sausage Roll

1 pound bulk pork sausage
2 cups chopped apples
2 cups bread crumbs
1 small onion, chopped

Roll sausage on waxed paper into ½-inch-thick rectangle. Combine apples, bread crumbs and onion in bowl and mix well. Spread over sausage. Roll as for jelly roll, sealing edge and ends. Place in baking dish. Bake at 350 degrees for 45 minutes or until sausage is cooked through.

Yield: 8 servings

Sausage Breakfast Bake

2 cups pancake mix
1¼ cups milk
2 eggs
1 tablespoon vegetable oil
1 (8-ounce) package brown and serve
   sausage links
1 (14-ounce) jar spiced apple rings
⅓ cup sugar
4 teaspoons cornstarch
1 tablespoon butter
¾ cup maple-flavored syrup

Combine pancake mix, milk, eggs and oil in bowl; beat with rotary beater. Pour into greased 9x13-inch baking dish. Cut sausage links into halves crosswise. Drain apple rings, reserving liquid. Arrange apple rings and sausages in serving portions on top of batter. Bake at 350 degrees for 30 to 35 minutes or until set. Add enough water to reserved apple ring liquid to measure ⅔ cup. Mix sugar and cornstarch in saucepan. Stir in apple ring liquid mixture. Cook until thickened, stirring constantly. Cook for 1 minute longer. Stir in butter and maple syrup. Pour sauce over baked layers. Serve immediately.

Yield: 6 servings

Sausage and Apple Rings

24 ounces bulk pork sausage
4 large cooking apples, cored
2/3 cup sugar
1 teaspoon cinnamon
1/4 cup butter or margarine
1/4 cup chopped fresh parsley

Shape sausage into twelve 1/4-inch-thick patties. Cook in skillet over medium heat for 10 to 15 minutes or until brown on both sides, turning once. Remove to warm plate; drain and wipe skillet. Cut ends off apples; cut each apple into 3 slices. Coat with mixture of sugar and cinnamon. Brown a few at a time in butter in killet, turning frequently and sprinkling with remaining sugar mixture. Place on sausage patties. Top with parsley.

Yield: 12 servings

Sausage Apple Sauerkraut

1 pound bulk pork sausage
2 tablespoons chopped onion
1 apple, peeled, sliced
2 cups sauerkraut
$1/2$ teaspoon caraway seeds
2 cups mashed potatoes
$1/3$ cup shredded Cheddar cheese
Paprika to taste

Brown sausage in skillet; drain, reserving 2 tablespoons drippings. Sauté onion in reserved drippings. Layer sausage, onion, apple and sauerkraut in $1^1/2$-quart casserole. Sprinkle with caraway seeds. Spread potatoes over top. Sprinkle with cheese and paprika. Bake at 350 degrees for 35 minutes or until golden brown.

Yield: 6 servings

Sausage, Cabbage and Apples

1 pound bulk pork sausage
1 tablespoon vinegar
1 medium head cabbage, shredded
3 apples, sliced
Salt to taste

Shape sausage into patties. Sauté sausage in skillet until brown and cooked through. Drain. Deglaze skillet with vinegar. Alternate layers of cabbage and apples in greased 8-inch square baking dish, salting lightly after each layer. Arrange sausage patties on top. Pour pan drippings over sausage. Bake, covered, at 350 degrees for 45 minutes or until apples are tender.

Variation: Substitute 4 cooked sliced sweet potatoes for cabbage

Yield: 6 servings

Baked Apples

Golden Delicious apples
Pineapple juice

Cut apples in half crosswise and remove core. Arrange in baking pan. Add enough pineapple juice to cover apples. Bake at 350 degrees until tender.

Yield: Variable

Make tasty Fruit Kabobs by threading apple chunks, banana chunks and seedless grapes alternately onto skewers. Baste with a mixture of melted butter, brown sugar and orange juice. Grill just until sugar has begun to crystallize but fruit is still crisp.

Buttery Cinnamon Skillet Apples

⅓ cup butter
1 tablespoon cornstarch
½ to ¾ cup sugar
¼ to ½ teaspoon cinnamon
4 medium apples, halved, cored

Melt butter in saucepan over medium heat. Add cornstarch and enough sugar to sweeten and mix well. Add cinnamon and apples. Cook, covered, over medium heat for 12 to 15 minutes or until apples are tender, basting apples with sauce occasionally. Arrange 2 apple halves in each of 4 serving dishes. Spoon sauce over each half.

Yield: 4 servings

Apple Cheese Casserole

2 (16-ounce) cans sliced apples
1 pound Velveeta cheese, cubed
¾ cup all-purpose flour
1 cup sugar
½ cup butter

Place apples in greased 3-quart casserole. Layer cheese, flour and sugar over apples. Dot with butter. Bake at 350 degrees for 30 to 40 minutes.

Yield: 8 servings

Peel, quarter and slice apples a few at a time; drop immediately into cool, lightly salted water. Spoon apples into a freezer container. Freeze immediately. Salt water prevents apples from darkening.

Cranapple Casserole

3 cups chopped peeled apples
2 cups cranberries
2 tablespoons all-purpose flour
1 cup sugar
³/₄ cup chopped pecans
¹/₂ cup all-purpose flour
3 envelopes cinnamon or apple
    instant oatmeal mix
¹/₂ cup packed light brown sugar
¹/₂ cup melted margarine

Combine apples, cranberries and 2 tablespoons flour in bowl and toss to coat. Add sugar and mix well. Spoon into greased 2-quart casserole. Combine pecans, ¹/₂ cup flour, oatmeal mix and brown sugar in bowl. Add margarine and mix well. Spoon over fruit. Bake at 350 degrees for 45 minutes.

Yield: 8 to 10 servings

For an Easy Cranberry Relish, grind together 1 package of cranberries, 4 red apples, 1 seeded orange and 2 cups of sugar. It will keep in the refrigerator for weeks.

Grandma's Mincemeat

1½ pounds chuck or sirloin
1 cup suet
3 cups finely chopped peeled apples
1 cup vinegar
1 cup molasses
3 cups sugar
1 teaspoon ground cloves
1 teaspoon cinnamon
1 teaspoon allspice
¾ pound citron or mixed peel
2 cups raisins

Braise beef until tender. Cool. Put cooked beef and suet through food chopper. Combine apples, vinegar, molasses, sugar, cloves, cinnamon and allspice in saucepan. Simmer over low heat until apples are tender. Add beef mixture, citron and raisins. Simmer over low heat for 1½ hours.

Yield: 6 cups

Holiday Stuffing

²/₃ cup chopped onion
1 cup chopped celery
²/₃ cup butter or margarine
Salt and pepper to taste
2¹/₂ teaspoons poultry seasoning
10 cups bread cubes
¹/₂ cup golden raisins
1 large apple, chopped
¹/₂ cup chopped almonds, toasted
1¹/₂ cups chicken broth

Sauté onion and celery in butter in skillet until tender. Add salt, pepper and poultry seasoning. Combine bread cubes, raisins, apple and almonds in large bowl and mix well. Stir in onion mixture. Pour in broth, stirring well. Spoon into large 5-quart baking pan. Bake at 325 degrees for 1 hour.

Yield: 36 servings

Spicy Peanut Sauce over Veggie Kabobs

1 onion, sliced
2 tablespoons peanut oil
3 cloves of garlic, pressed
8 ounces peanut butter
Juice of 1 lemon
Red hot pepper sauce to taste
2 tablespoons soy sauce
1 tablespoon brown sugar
1 cup water
3 onions, coarsely chopped
1 (8-ounce) can pineapple chunks
2 tomatoes, quartered
10 small mushrooms
1/2 head broccoli, cut into chunks
2 apples, cut into chunks
2 green or red bell peppers, cut into chunks
1/4 to 1/2 cup peanut oil
1/4 to 1/2 cup soy sauce

Sauté sliced onion in 2 tablespoons peanut oil in skillet. Add garlic, peanut butter, lemon juice, hot sauce, 2 tablespoons soy sauce, brown sugar and water and mix well. Cook until mixture is of creamy consistency, stirring constantly and adding additional water if needed. Thread coarsely chopped onion, pineapple, tomatoes, mushrooms, broccoli, apples and green peppers alternately onto metal or bamboo skewers. Brush with mixture of 1/4 cup peanut oil and 1/4 cup soy sauce. Grill or broil kabobs, turning to brown on all sides. Serve with peanut sauce.

Yield: 6 servings

Apple Butter

5 pounds Granny Smith apples, peeled,
  chopped
3 cups water
3 cups sugar
3 cups packed dark brown sugar
1 (1³⁄₄-ounce) package powdered pectin
1 tablespoon cinnamon
1 teaspoon allspice
¹⁄₄ teaspoon ground cloves
¹⁄₄ teaspoon nutmeg

Combine apples and water in large saucepan. Bring to a boil. Simmer for 20 to 25 minutes or until tender. Mash apples. Stir in sugar, brown sugar, pectin, cinnamon, allspice, cloves and nutmeg. Bring to a boil. Cook for 2 minutes, stirring constantly. Pour mixture into 6 hot sterilized jars, leaving ¹⁄₄-inch headspace. Seal with 2-piece lids. Process in boiling water bath for 5 minutes.

Yield: 6 pints

Slow-Cooker Apple Butter

3 (16-ounce) cans Apple Barn™
  applesauce
1 tablespoon cinnamon
3 cups sugar
1 teaspoon ground cloves
1¹⁄₂ teaspoons lemon juice

Combine applesauce, cinnamon, sugar, cloves and lemon juice in slow cooker and mix well. Cook on High for 8 to 10 hours or on Low for 16 to 20 hours. Remove cover during final hours of cooking to cook to desired thickness.

Yield: 32 servings

Apple Bread

½ cup margarine
1 cup sugar
2 eggs
2 tablespoons sour milk
1 teaspoon baking soda
½ teaspoon salt
2 cups all-purpose flour
2 cups chopped apples
2 tablespoons granulated sugar
2 tablespoons all-purpose flour
1 tablespoon cinnamon
2 tablespoons margarine

Cream ½ cup margarine and 1 cup sugar in bowl until light and fluffy. Beat in eggs and milk. Add baking soda, salt and 2 cups flour and mix well. Stir in apples. Pour into greased loaf pan. Combine 2 tablespoons sugar, 2 tablespoons flour and cinnamon in bowl and mix well. Cut in margarine until crumbly. Sprinkle over top of batter. Bake at 325 degrees for 15 minutes. Reduce heat to 300 degrees. Bake for 1 hour or until golden brown.

Note: To make sour milk, add 1 tablespoon lemon juice or vinegar to 1 cup milk.

Yield: 1 loaf

Cinnamon Apple Swirl Bread

½ cup scalded milk
1 cup sugar
2 teaspoons salt
¼ cup butter
2 envelopes yeast
½ cup warm water
2 eggs
4 to 4½ cups all-purpose flour
⅔ cup sugar
1 tablespoon flour
2 teaspoons cinnamon
1½ cups finely diced apples
⅓ cup chopped walnuts
2 tablespoons butter, softened
1 cup confectioners' sugar
1 to 2 tablespoons apple juice

Combine milk, ⅓ cup sugar, salt and ¼ cup butter in saucepan over medium heat, stirring until butter melts. Cool to lukewarm. Dissolve yeast in warm water in large bowl. Stir in milk mixture and eggs. Gradually stir in enough flour to form stiff dough. Knead on floured surface until smooth and satiny. Place in greased bowl, turning to coat surface. Let rise, covered, in warm place until doubled in bulk. Combine ⅔ cup sugar, 1 tablespoon of flour and cinnamon in bowl and mix well. Toss apples and walnuts in sugar mixture. Roll dough into 11x15-inch rectangle on lightly floured surface. Spread with 2 tablespoons softened butter. Top with apple mixture. Roll as for jelly roll, starting with 15-inch side. Seal edge and ends. Cut into halves. Place each half in greased 5x9-inch loaf pan. Cut about ½-inch deep with scissors into 10 slices. Let rise, covered, until doubled in bulk. Bake at 350 degrees for 40 minutes or until golden brown. Remove from pans. Mix confectioners' sugar and apple juice in bowl. Drizzle icing over loaves.

Yield: 2 loaves

Fresh Apple Loaf

4 cups chopped apples
1 cup chopped pecans
2 cups sugar
3 cups all-purpose flour
2 teaspoons baking soda
¼ teaspoon salt
¼ teaspoon nutmeg
¼ teaspoon ground cloves
¾ teaspoon cinnamon
1 cup melted butter
2 teaspoons vanilla extract
2 eggs, lightly beaten

Toss apples and pecans in sugar in bowl. Let stand for 1 hour, stirring often. Combine flour, baking soda, salt, nutmeg, cloves and cinnamon in large bowl and mix well. Add apple mixture and mix well. Stir in butter, vanilla and eggs. Pour into 2 greased and floured loaf pans. Bake at 325 degrees for 1 hour or until loaves test done. Cool in pans for 10 minutes. Remove to wire rack to cool completely.

Yield: 2 loaves

Apple Loaf Bread

1 cup vegetable oil
3 eggs
2 cups sugar
1 teaspoon salt
1 teaspoon cinnamon
1 teaspoon baking soda
3 cups all-purpose flour
1 cups chopped nuts
3 cups chopped apples

Combine oil and eggs and mix well. Add sugar, salt, cinnamon, baking soda and flour and mix well. Stir in nuts and apples. Pour into 2 greased 5x9-inch loaf pans. Bake at 300 degrees for 1½ hours.

Note: For a moister loaf bake for a shorter time.

Yield: 2 loaves

Apple Muffins

2 cups self-rising flour
1/2 cup sugar
1 1/2 teaspoons cinnamon
1 egg
1 cup milk
1 cup chopped apples
2 tablespoons corn oil
1 cup chopped English walnuts

Sift flour, sugar and cinnamon in large bowl. Beat egg in medium bowl. Add milk, apples, corn oil and nuts and mix well. Add to dry ingredients and stir just until mixed. Fill greased muffin cups 2/3 full. Bake at 425 degrees for 15 to 20 minutes or until golden brown. Serve hot.

Yield: 12 muffins

The first American apple orchard was planted on Beacon Hill, overlooking Boston Harbor, in the early 1600s. It is said that this orchard was planted by William Blaxton, founder of Boston.

Oatmeal Apple Muffins

1 cup quick-cooking oats
1 tablespoon baking powder
1 teaspoon nutmeg
1 cup all-purpose flour
1/3 cup sugar
1 teaspoon salt
2 teaspoons cinnamon
1 egg, beaten
1/2 cup vegetable oil
3/4 cup milk
1 cup raisins
1 apple, chopped

Combine oats, baking powder, nutmeg, flour, sugar, salt and cinnamon in medium bowl. Combine egg, oil and milk in bowl and mix well. Add to dry ingredients and stir just until mixed. Fold in raisins and apple. Fill greased muffin cups 2/3 full. Bake at 400 degrees for 15 to 20 minutes or until golden brown.

Yield: 12 muffins

Apple Pancakes with Cider Syrup

Pancakes
2 cups baking mix
1/2 teaspoon cinnamon
1 egg
1 1/3 cups milk
3/4 cup grated apple
Cider Syrup

Combine baking mix, cinnamon, egg and milk in mixer bowl and beat until smooth. Fold in apple. Pour 1/4 cup at a time onto hot lightly greased griddle. Bake until both sides are golden brown, turning once. Serve with Cider Syrup.

Cider Syrup
1 cup sugar
2 tablespoons cornstarch
1/2 teaspoon pumpkin pie spice
2 cups apple cider
2 tablespoons lemon juice
1/4 cup butter

Combine sugar, cornstarch and pumpkin pie spice in saucepan and mix well. Stir in cider and lemon juice. Cook over low heat until mixture thickens, stirring constantly. Bring to a boil and boil for 1 minute. Remove from heat. Add butter and stir until melted.

Yield: 18 pancakes

Make Ahead Apple and Nut Pancakes

1½ cups buttermilk
3 eggs, lightly beaten
2 cups all-purpose flour
1 tablespoon sugar
1 tablespoon baking powder
½ teaspoon salt
½ teaspoon baking soda
½ cup melted butter
1½ cups finely chopped apples
½ cup chopped nuts

Combine buttermilk and eggs in bowl and mix well. Add flour, sugar, baking powder, salt and baking soda and mix well. Stir in butter. Stir in apples and nuts. Chill, covered, in refrigerator for 2 hours or more. Pour ¼ cup at a time onto hot lightly greased griddle. Bake until golden brown on both sides, turning once.

Yield: 16 to 20 pancakes

To prevent shriveling of apples and transferring of odors, store small quantities in plastic bags in the refrigerator. Store large quantities in a cool, dark airy place. Sort occasionally to remove those with signs of spoilage.

Cakes

The Creamery's shakes, sodas and ice cream sundaes will bring out the kid in everyone.

Apple Cake

Cake

3 cups chopped tart apples
1½ cups canola oil
1 cup sugar
½ cup firmly packed brown sugar
2 teaspoons vanilla extract
3 eggs
3 cups self-rising flour
1 tablespoon cinnamon
1 teaspoon nutmeg
½ teaspoon ground cloves
1 cup chopped walnuts or pecans
Glaze

Soak apples in lightly salted water in bowl for several minutes. Beat canola oil, sugar, brown sugar and vanilla in mixer bowl until smooth. Add eggs 1 at a time, mixing well after each addition. Sift flour, cinnamon, nutmeg and cloves together in bowl. Add to sugar mixture and beat until smooth. Drain apples. Stir apples and walnuts into batter. Pour into greased and floured bundt pan. Bake at 325 degrees for 1 hour and 30 minutes or until wooden pick inserted in cake comes out clean. Cool in pan for 15 to 20 minutes. Invert onto wire rack to cool completely. Place on cake plate. Drizzle Glaze over cake.

Glaze

3 tablespoons butter or margarine
3 tablespoons firmly packed brown sugar
3 tablespoons sugar
3 tablespoons milk
½ teaspoon vanilla extract

Combine butter, brown sugar, sugar, milk and vanilla in saucepan. Cook over medium heat until glaze boils, stirring constantly. Boil for 1 minute. Let stand to cool slightly.

Yield: 16 servings

Butterscotch Apple Cake

2 cups sugar
1 cup vegetable oil
4 eggs
3/4 teaspoon cinnamon
2 1/2 cups self-rising flour
3 cups chopped tart apples
Butterscotch chips to taste
1 cup chopped pecans

Combine sugar, oil and eggs in bowl and mix well. Add cinnamon and flour and mix well. Stir in apples. Pour into greased 9x13-inch baking pan. Sprinkle top with butterscotch chips and pecans. Bake at 350 degrees for 35 to 40 minutes or until wooden pick inserted in center comes out clean.

Yield: 15 servings

Eat an apple everyday to boost your energy level. Eating an apple instead of a candy bar not only gives you an energy boost, but it will also prevent the quick blood-sugar peak that candy gives because it take longer for your body to digest the apple. While the candy bar contains more calories and fat than you need, the apple is a fat-free healthy snack.

Caramel Apple Cake

Cake

1½ cups vegetable oil
1½ cups sugar
½ cup firmly packed brown sugar
3 eggs
3 cups all-purpose flour
2 teaspoons cinnamon
½ teaspoon nutmeg
1 teaspoon baking soda
½ teaspoon salt
3½ cups peeled chopped apples
1 cup chopped walnuts
2 teaspoons vanilla extract
Caramel Icing
Chopped walnuts to taste

*M*ix oil, sugar and brown sugar in mixer bowl. Mix until smooth. Add the eggs 1 at a time, mixing well after each addition. Combine flour, cinnamon, nutmeg, baking soda and salt in bowl and mix well. Add dry ingredients to sugar mixture and mix well. Fold in apples, 1 cup walnuts and vanilla. Pour batter into greased and floured 10-inch tube pan. Bake at 325 degrees for 1½ hours or until cake tests done. Cool in pan for 10 minutes. Invert onto wire rack to cool completely. Place on a cake plate. Drizzle Caramel Icing over cake. Sprinkle with walnuts.

Caramel Icing

½ cup firmly packed brown sugar
⅓ cup light cream
¼ cup butter or margarine
⅛ teaspoon salt
1 cup confectioners' sugar

Heat brown sugar, cream, butter and salt in top of double boiler until sugar dissolves. Let stand at room temperature until cool. Add confectioners' sugar and mix until smooth.

Yield: 16 servings

Coconut Apple Cake

2 cups sugar
1¼ cups vegetable oil
3 eggs
3 cups all-purpose flour
1 teaspoon baking soda
1 teaspoon salt
2 teaspoons baking powder
1 cup flaked coconut
2 cups chopped apples
1 cup chopped pecans
2 teaspoons vanilla extract

Beat sugar, oil and eggs in mixer bowl until smooth. Add flour, baking soda, salt and baking powder and mix well. Stir in coconut, apples, pecans and vanilla. Pour into greased tube pan. Bake at 350 degrees for 1 hour and 15 minutes or until cake tests done.

Yield: 16 servings

Dried Apple Cake

2 cups chopped dried apples
1 cup sugar
1 cup cane sugar syrup
1 cup shortening
1 cup milk
1 teaspoon baking soda
3 cups all-purpose flour
$1/2$ teaspoon salt
1 teaspoon allspice
1 teaspoon cinnamon
2 cups raisins
1 cup chopped pecans
1 egg, beaten

Soak apples in water in bowl for 1 hour or until soft. Drain. Combine apples, sugar and syrup in 4-quart saucepan. Heat to rolling boil. Cook over medium heat for 20 minutes, stirring frequently. Remove from heat. Add shortening, milk and baking soda to apple mixture, stirring until shortening melts. Sift flour, salt, allspice and cinnamon together. Stir dry ingredients into apple mixture. Add raisins and pecans and mix well. Fold in beaten egg. Pour batter into greased and floured tube pan. Bake at 350 degrees for 1 hour and 10 minutes or until cake pulls from sides of pan. Cool in pan on wire rack for 10 minutes. Invert onto wire rack to cool completely.

Note: Store cake wrapped in foil and it will stay moist for days.

Yield: 16 servings

Fresh Apple Cake

Cake
1 1/2 cups sugar
2 eggs
3 cups chopped apples
1 1/2 teaspoons baking soda
1/2 teaspoon nutmeg
1/2 teaspoon cinnamon
1 1/2 cups all-purpose flour
Topping

Combine sugar and eggs in large bowl and mix well. Stir in apples. Combine baking soda, nutmeg, cinnamon and flour in bowl and mix well. Add dry ingredients to apple mixture and mix well. Pour into ungreased 9x13-inch baking pan. Bake at 325 degrees for 1 hour or until wooden pick inserted in center comes out clean. Pour Topping over hot cake.

Topping
1/2 cup sugar
1/2 cup firmly packed brown sugar
2 tablespoons all-purpose flour
1/2 teaspoon salt
1 cup water
1 teaspoon vanilla extract
1 tablespoon butter

Combine sugar, brown sugar, flour, salt and water in small saucepan. Cook until sugar mixture boils and starts to thicken, stirring constantly. Remove from heat. Add vanilla and butter, stirring until butter melts.

Yield: 15 servings

Sir Isaac Newton is said to have discovered the law of gravity when an apple fell on his head.

Fresh Apple Cake with Brown Sugar Topping

Cake
1 1/2 cups vegetable oil
2 cups sugar
3 eggs
3 cups self-rising flour, sifted
1/2 teaspoon cinnamon
3 cups chopped apples
1 1/2 cups chopped pecans
1 teaspoon vanilla extract
Brown Sugar Topping

Beat oil, sugar and eggs in mixer bowl until smooth. Add flour and cinnamon and mix well. Fold in apples, pecans and vanilla. Pour into greased and floured tube pan. Bake at 350 degrees for 45 minutes or until cake tests done. Pour Brown Sugar Topping over cake. Bake for 10 minutes.

Brown Sugar Topping
1 cup firmly packed light brown sugar
1/2 cup butter
1 teaspoon vanilla extract
1/4 cup milk

Combine brown sugar, butter, vanilla and milk in small saucepan. Cook over medium heat for 2 1/2 minutes, stirring constantly.

Yield: 16 servings

Apple Bundt Cake

4 cups chopped apples
2 cups sugar
1 cup vegetable oil
2 eggs, well beaten
1 teaspoon vanilla extract
1 cup chopped nuts
3 cups all-purpose flour
½ teaspoon baking soda
½ teaspoon salt
1 teaspoon nutmeg
1 teaspoon cinnamon

Combine apples and sugar in large bowl. Let stand for 1 hour, stirring often. Add oil, eggs, vanilla and nuts and mix well. Combine flour, baking soda, salt, nutmeg and cinnamon in bowl and mix well. Add dry ingredients to apple mixture, mixing well. Pour batter into tube pan. Bake at 350 degrees for 1 hour and 15 minutes or until cake tests done.

Yield: 16 servings

Apple Nut Cake

2 cups sugar
1½ cups vegetable oil
2 eggs
3 cups all-purpose flour
1 teaspoon baking soda
½ teaspoon salt
1 teaspoon cinnamon
1 teaspoon nutmeg
3 cups chopped apples
1 cup chopped nuts

Combine sugar, oil and eggs in large bowl and mix well. Sift flour, baking soda, salt, cinnamon and nutmeg together. Add dry ingredients to sugar mixture and mix well. Fold in apples and nuts. Pour batter into greased and floured 9x13-inch baking pan. Bake at 350 degrees for 30 to 40 minutes or until wooden pick inserted in center comes out clean.

Yield: 15 servings

Countryside Apple Cake

1 cup vegetable oil
2 eggs
2 cups sugar
1 teaspoon vanilla extract
1 teaspoon cinnamon
3 cups self-rising flour
1 cup chopped apples

Combine oil, eggs, sugar and vanilla in bowl and mix well. Combine cinnamon and flour in bowl and mix well. Stir flour mixture into sugar mixture. Fold in apples. Pour batter into greased and floured tube pan. Bake at 350 degrees for 1 hour or until cake tests done.

Yield: 16 servings

Fresh Apple Sheet Cake

1 cup vegetable oil
1⅓ cups sugar
4 eggs
2 cups all-purpose flour
1 teaspoon baking powder
1 teaspoon cinnamon
1 teaspoon vanilla extract
5 large apples, peeled, sliced
¼ cup chopped nuts

Combine oil and sugar in bowl and mix well. Add eggs 1 at a time, mixing well after each addition. Add flour, baking powder and cinnamon and mix well. Fold in vanilla, apples and nuts. Pour batter into greased 9x13 inch baking pan. Bake at 375 degrees for 45 minutes or until wooden pick inserted in center comes out clean.

Yield: 15 servings

Glazed Apple Cake

Cake
2 eggs
³/₄ cup vegetable oil
1¹/₂ cups sugar
2 cups chopped apples
2 cups chopped nuts
2 cups all-purpose flour
1 teaspoon baking soda
2 teaspoons cinnamon
2 teaspoons vanilla extract
Sugar Glaze

Combine eggs, oil and sugar in bowl and mix well. Stir in apples and nuts. Add flour, baking soda, cinnamon and vanilla and mix well. Pour batter into greased and floured 9x13-inch baking pan. Bake at 350 degrees for 35 minutes or until cake tests done. Pour Sugar Glaze over hot cake.

Sugar Glaze
1 cup sugar
¹/₄ cup margarine
¹/₄ cup milk

Combine sugar, margarine and milk in small saucepan. Cook until mixture boils, stirring constantly.

Yield: 15 servings

Old-Fashioned Fresh Apple Cake

4 eggs
$^3/_4$ cup sugar
$^3/_4$ cup vegetable oil
2 cups all-purpose flour
1$^1/_2$ teaspoons baking powder
4 apples, peeled, shredded
1 cup chopped nuts

Combine eggs, sugar and oil in bowl and mix well. Add flour and baking powder and mix well. Fold in apples and nuts. Pour batter into greased 9x13-inch baking pan. Bake at 375 degrees for 45 minutes or until wooden pick inserted in center comes out clean.

Yield: 15 servings

If a recipe calls for one pound of apples, you will need 4 small apples, 3 medium apples, or 2 large apples. One pound is also equal to 2$^3/_4$ cups of sliced apples or 1$^1/_2$ cups grated apples.

Apple Walnut Cake

2 cups sugar
1/2 cup margarine
2 eggs
2 cups all-purpose flour
2 teaspoons cinnamon
2 teaspoons nutmeg
1 teaspoon salt
2 teaspoons baking soda
1 1/2 cups chopped walnuts
6 apples, finely chopped

Cream sugar and margarine in bowl until light and fluffy. Add eggs 1 at a time, beating well after each addition. Combine flour, cinnamon, nutmeg, salt and baking soda in bowl and mix well. Add dry ingredients to sugar mixture and mix well. Fold in walnuts and apples. Pour batter into greased 9x13-inch baking pan. Bake at 325 degrees for 40 to 45 minutes or until wooden pick inserted in center comes out clean.

Yield: 15 servings

Knobby Apple Cake

3 tablespoons butter
1 cup sugar
1 egg, beaten
1 cup all-purpose flour
1 teaspoon baking soda
1/2 teaspoon salt
1/2 teaspoon nutmeg
1/2 teaspoon cinnamon
3 cups chopped apples
1/2 cup chopped nuts
1 teaspoon vanilla extract

Cream butter and sugar in bowl until light and fluffy. Add egg, beating well. Sift flour, baking soda, salt, nutmeg and cinnamon together. Add dry ingredients to sugar mixture, mixing well. Stir in apples, nuts and vanilla. Pour batter into 8x8-inch baking pan. Bake at 350 degrees for 40 to 45 minutes or until wooden pick inserted in center comes out clean.

Yield: 9 servings

"The Big Apple" is a term coined by the jazz musicians of the 1930s to mean large city. It was not until the 1970s that it replaced New York City's previous nickname of "Fun City."

Apple Oatmeal Cake

1¼ cups boiling water
1 cup quick-cooking oats
½ cup margarine, softened
1 cup sugar
1 cup firmly packed brown sugar
2 eggs
1 teaspoon vanilla extract
1 cup peeled, chopped apples
1¾ cups all-purpose flour
1 teaspoon baking soda
½ teaspoon salt
½ teaspoon cinnamon
1 (16-ounce) can coconut pecan frosting

Pour boiling water over oats in bowl. Let stand, covered, for 20 minutes. Cream margarine, sugar and brown sugar in mixer bowl until light and fluffy. Add eggs and vanilla and beat until smooth. Add oatmeal mixture and apples and mix well. Sift flour, baking soda, salt and cinnamon together. Add to apple mixture and mix well. Pour batter into greased and floured 9x9-inch baking pan. Bake at 350 degrees for 50 minutes or until wooden pick inserted in center comes out clean. Let stand in pan on wire rack to cool completely. Spread coconut pecan frosting over cake.

Yield: 9 servings

Old-Fashioned Chopped Apple Cake

2 cups sugar
²/₃ cup shortening
3 eggs
1²/₃ teaspoons baking soda
1 cup coffee
2¹/₂ cups all-purpose flour
1 teaspoon nutmeg
1 teaspoon cinnamon
1 teaspoon allspice
1 teaspoon salt
2 teaspoons vanilla extract
1 cup raisins
3 to 4 cups chopped apples
1 cup chopped dates
²/₃ cup chopped nuts

Cream sugar and shortening in mixer bowl until light and fluffy. Add eggs 1 at a time, beating well after each addition. Dissolve baking soda in coffee. Add to sugar mixture. Combine flour, nutmeg, cinnamon, allspice and salt in bowl and mix well. Add dry ingredients to coffee mixture and mix well. Stir in vanilla, raisins, apples, dates and nuts. Pour batter into greased and floured 9x13-inch cake pan. Bake at 350 degrees for 1 hour or until wooden pick inserted in center comes out clean.

Yield: 15 servings

Apple-Walnut Cake with Cream Cheese Frosting

Cake
1⅔ cups sugar
2 eggs
½ cup vegetable oil
2 teaspoons vanilla extract
2 cups all-purpose flour
2 teaspoons baking soda
1½ teaspoons cinnamon
1 teaspoon salt
½ teaspoon nutmeg
4 cups chopped apples
1 cup chopped walnuts
Cream Cheese Frosting

Beat sugar and eggs in mixer bowl until smooth. Add oil and vanilla and mix well. Combine flour, baking soda, cinnamon, salt and nutmeg in bowl and mix well. Add dry ingredients to sugar mixture and mix well. Stir in apples and walnuts. Pour batter into greased 9x13-inch baking pan. Bake at 350 degrees for 50 to 55 minutes or until cake tests done. Let stand on wire rack to cool completely. Spread Cream Cheese Frosting over the cake.

Cream Cheese Frosting
6 ounces cream cheese, softened
3 tablespoons margarine or butter
1 teaspoon vanilla extract
1½ cups confectioners' sugar

Beat cream cheese, margarine and vanilla in mixer bowl until smooth. Add confectioners' sugar, beating until frosting reaches spreading consistency.

Yield: 15 servings

Applesauce Cake

1 cup sugar
¼ cup shortening
1 cup Apple Barn™ applesauce
1 cup sour milk
1 teaspoon baking soda
2 cups all-purpose flour
⅛ teaspoon salt
2 teaspoons (heaping) baking powder
Ground cloves to taste
Cinnamon to taste
½ cup chopped nuts
½ cup raisins

Cream sugar and shortening in mixer bowl until light and fluffy. Add applesauce and sour milk and mix well. Combine baking soda, flour, salt, baking powder, cloves and cinnamon in bowl and mix well. Add to sugar mixture, mixing well. Fold in nuts and raisins. Pour batter into 9x13-inch baking pan. Bake at 350 degrees for 35 to 40 minutes or until cake tests done.

Note: To make sour milk, add 1 tablespoon lemon juice or vinegar to 1 cup milk.

Yield: 15 servings

"Keep me as the apple of your eye; Hide me under the shadow of your wings." Psalms 17:8.

Applesauce Spice Cake

1 (15-ounce) box raisins
1½ cups black walnuts
1 cup all-purpose flour
1 cup butter
2 cups sugar
3 cups all-purpose flour
2 teaspoons baking soda
1 tablespoon nutmeg
1 tablespoon cinnamon
2 cups cooked dried apples

Combine raisins and walnuts in bowl. Add 1 cup flour, tossing to coat raisins and walnuts. Cream butter and sugar in mixer bowl until light and fluffy. Add 3 cups flour, baking soda, nutmeg and cinnamon and mix well. Stir in apples. Pour into bundt pan. Bake at 325 degrees for 1 hour or until cake tests done.

Note: This cake is best when cooked about a week before you plan to eat it.

Yield: 16 servings

Brown Sugar Applesauce Cake

1 cup butter
2 cups Apple Barn™ applesauce
2 cups firmly packed dark brown sugar
4 teaspoons baking soda
4 cups all-purpose flour
1/2 teaspoon salt
1 teaspoon allspice
1 teaspoon cinnamon
1 teaspoon nutmeg
1 teaspoon mace
2 cups raisins
1 cup chopped black walnuts

Cook butter, applesauce, brown sugar and baking soda in large saucepan until butter is melted, stirring constantly. Add flour, salt, allspice, cinnamon, nutmeg and mace and mix well. Stir in raisins and walnuts. Pour into 1 tube pan or 2 loaf pans. Bake at 350 degrees for 45 to 60 minutes or until cake tests done.

Yield: 16 servings

Chocolate Applesauce Cake

½ cup shortening
½ cup firmly packed brown sugar
1 cup sugar
2 eggs
2½ cups Apple Barn™ applesauce
2 cups all-purpose flour
2 tablespoons baking cocoa
1½ teaspoons baking soda
¾ teaspoon salt
½ teaspoon cinnamon
½ teaspoon ground cloves
½ teaspoon nutmeg
½ teaspoon allspice
¾ cup raisins, nuts or dates

Cream shortening, brown sugar and sugar in mixer bowl until light and fluffy. Add eggs and applesauce and mix well. Sift flour, baking cocoa, baking soda, salt, cinnamon, cloves, nutmeg and allspice together. Add dry ingredients to sugar mixture, mixing well. Stir in raisins. Pour into greased and floured 9x13-inch pan. Bake at 350 degrees for 55 to 60 minutes or until wooden pick inserted in center comes out clean.

Yield: 15 servings

Applesauce Cupcakes

1¼ cups sifted cake flour
⅔ cup sugar
1¾ teaspoons baking powder
½ teaspoon salt
1 teaspoon baking soda
¼ teaspoon cinnamon
⅔ cup Apple Barn™ applesauce
½ cup milk
1 teaspoon vanilla extract
1 egg, beaten

Sift flour, sugar, baking powder, salt, baking soda and cinnamon together in large bowl. Mix applesauce, milk, vanilla and egg in large bowl. Add applesauce mixture to dry ingredients and stir until blended. Spoon batter into paper-lined muffin cups. Bake at 375 degrees for 18 to 20 minutes or until puffed and golden brown.

Yield: 12 cupcakes

Out of 10 billion pounds of apples grown annually, 57 percent are eaten fresh and 43 percent are processed. In the processing, 53 percent are pressed as juice and cider, 29 percent are cooked as applesauce.

Apple Stack Cake

3 cups all-purpose flour
1 tablespoon baking powder
1½ cups sugar
1 cup vegetable oil
4 eggs
⅓ cup orange juice
2½ teaspoons vanilla extract
1 teaspoon cinnamon
½ cup sugar
4 apples, thinly sliced

Sift flour, baking powder and 1½ cups sugar into large mixer bowl. Make a well in center. Add oil, eggs, orange juice and vanilla. Beat for 4 minutes or until smooth and very thick; do not underbeat. Combine cinnamon and ½ cup sugar in small bowl. Layer batter, apple slices and cinnamon mixture ⅓ at a time in greased and floured 10-inch tube pan. Bake at 350 degrees for 1 hour and 15 minutes or until cake tests done. Cool in pan for 15 minutes. Invert onto cake plate. Cool completely before serving.

Yield: 16 servings

Stack Cake

Cake

2 cups sugar
1 cup butter or shortening
2 eggs
6 cups all-purpose flour
1 teaspoon baking soda
1 tablespoon baking powder
1/2 cup buttermilk
1 teaspoon vanilla extract
Apple Filling

Cream sugar and butter in mixer bowl until light and fluffy. Add eggs 1 at a time, mixing well after each addition. Sift flour, baking soda and baking powder together. Combine buttermilk and vanilla in small bowl and mix well. Add dry ingredients and buttermilk mixture alternately to sugar mixture, mixing well after each addition. Pour into 6 or 7 cake pans. Bake at 450 degrees for 10 to 12 minutes or until golden brown. Cool in pans for 10 minutes. Remove to wire rack to cool completely. Reserve 1 cake layer. Place 1 cake layer on plate. Spread with Apple Filling. Repeat with remaining layers and filling. Top with reserved cake layer.

Apple Filling

1 cup firmly packed brown sugar
1 cup sugar
2 teaspoons cinnamon
1/2 teaspoon ground cloves
1/2 teaspoon allspice
2 cups dried apples, cooked until tender

Combine brown sugar, sugar, cinnamon, cloves and allspice in bowl and mix well. Stir in apples.

Yield: 12 to 16 servings

Apple Cake from Cortina

½ cup unsalted butter
½ cup sugar
⅛ teaspoon salt
3 eggs
1½ cups all-purpose flour
1 teaspoon baking powder
1 tablespoon orange zest (optional)
¾ cup coarsely chopped walnuts (optional)
4 large tart apples, peeled, halved
1 tablespoon sugar
¼ teaspoon cinnamon

Butter 9-inch springform pan. Line with waxed paper. Cream butter, sugar and salt in mixer bowl until light and fluffy. Beat in eggs 1 at a time, mixing well after each addition. Sift flour and baking powder together. Add to creamed mixture, mixing well. Stir in orange zest and walnuts. Spread batter evenly in prepared pan. Cut each apple half into 3 or 4 wedges. Arrange wedges on sides on top of batter, keeping about ½ inch from side of pan and, overlapping slightly. Arrange remaining wedges in a fan pattern. Sprinkle with sugar and cinnamon. Bake on middle oven rack at 350 degrees for 40 minutes or until apples are deep golden brown and torta is firm to touch. Cool torta in pan for 5 minutes. Remove side of pan . Slide torta and waxed paper off base to a wire rack. Cool completely. Run spatula between torta and paper. Slide torta from waxed paper onto platter. Store torta, loosely covered, at room temperature.

Yield: 8 servings

Apple Breakfast Cake

1/3 cup sugar
2 teaspoons cinnamon
2 cups sugar
4 eggs
2 1/2 teaspoons vanilla extract
1 cup vegetable oil
1/2 cup orange juice
3 cups all-purpose flour
1 tablespoon baking powder
1/4 teaspoon salt
5 medium apples, peeled, chopped

Combine 1/3 cup sugar and cinnamon in bowl, mixing well. Set aside. Beat 2 cups sugar, eggs, vanilla, oil and orange juice in mixer bowl until smooth. Combine flour, baking powder and salt and mix well. Stir flour mixture into egg mixture until smooth. Spoon 1/2 of batter into greased and floured 10-inch bundt pan. Arrange apples evenly over batter. Sprinkle 1/2 of cinnamon mixture over apples. Pour remaining batter over apples. Sprinkle with remaining cinnamon mixture. Bake at 350 degrees for 1 hour or until cake tests done. Cool in pan on wire rack for 1 hour. Invert onto serving plate.

Yield: 16 servings

Apple Coffee Cake

Cake

1/2 cup butter
1 cup milk
1 egg
1 teaspoon vanilla extract
1 cup all-purpose flour
1 cup sugar
1/4 teaspoon cinnamon
1 teaspoon baking powder
1 (15-ounce) can Apple Barn™ apple
   pie filling, drained
Vanilla Icing

Melt butter in glass 8x8-inch or 8 1/2x11-inch baking dish. Combine milk, egg and vanilla in bowl and mix well. Add flour, sugar, cinnamon and baking powder and mix well. Pour over melted butter; do not mix. Arrange apples over top of batter. Bake at 350 degrees for 30 to 35 minutes or until light brown. Cool 10 minutes. Spread Vanilla Icing over cake.

Vanilla Icing

1/2 cup confectioners' sugar
1 tablespoon butter, softened
1/4 teaspoon vanilla extract
Milk to taste

Combine confectioners' sugar, butter, vanilla and enough milk to make of spreading consistency in bowl and mix well.

Yield: 9 servings

Apple Ring Coffee Cake

3 cups all-purpose flour
1 teaspoon salt
1 teaspoon cinnamon
1 cup coarsely chopped walnuts
1½ cups sugar
1 cup vegetable oil
2 teaspoons vanilla extract
2 eggs
2 medium tart apples, peeled, chopped

Sift flour, salt and cinnamon into large bowl. Stir in walnuts. Combine sugar, oil, vanilla and eggs in bowl and mix well. Stir in apples. Add sugar mixture to dry ingredients and stir just until moistened. Spoon batter into greased 10-inch tube pan. Bake at 325 degrees for 1 hour or until wooden pick inserted in center comes out clean. Cool in pan on wire rack for 10 minutes. Invert onto wire rack to cool completely. Garnish top of cake with confectioners' sugar sprinkled through fine-mesh sieve.

Yield: 12 to 16 servings

Eight varieties of apples account for 80 percent of American apple production. The favorites are, in order: Red Delicious, Golden Delicious, Granny Smith, McIntosh, Rome Beauty, Jonathan, York, and Stayman.

Country Apple Coffee Cake

Cake

1¹/₂ cups chopped peeled apples
1 (10-ounce) can flaky refrigerator
  biscuits
¹/₃ cup firmly packed brown sugar
¹/₄ teaspoon cinnamon
¹/₃ cup light corn syrup
1 tablespoon margarine
1¹/₂ teaspoons whiskey (optional)
1 egg
¹/₂ cup pecan halves or pieces
Glaze

Arrange 1 cup of apples in greased 9-inch cake pan. Cut each biscuit into 4 pieces. Arrange point side up over apples. Top with remaining ¹/₂ cup apples. Combine brown sugar, cinnamon, corn syrup, margarine, whiskey and egg in mixer bowl and beat for 2 minutes. Stir in pecans. Spoon sugar mixture over biscuits. Bake at 350 degrees for 35 to 45 minutes or until deep golden brown. Drizzle Glaze over warm cake. Store in refrigerator.

Glaze

¹/₃ cup confectioners' sugar
¹/₄ teaspoon vanilla extract
1 to 2 teaspoons milk

Combine confectioners' sugar, vanilla and enough milk to make of spreading consistency in bowl and mix well.

Yield: 6 to 8 servings

104

Buttermilk Glaze

1 cup sugar
1/2 teaspoon baking soda
1/2 cup buttermilk
1/2 cup margarine
1 teaspoon vanilla extract

Combine sugar, baking soda, buttermilk, margarine and vanilla in saucepan. Cook over medium heat for 3 minutes, stirring constantly. Poke holes in top of cake. Pour glaze over hot cake.

Yield: 1 cup glaze

Juice Glaze

1 cup confectioners' sugar
1 to 2 tablespoons apple or cherry juice

Combine confectioners' sugar and enough juice to make of desired consistency in bowl and mix well. Pour over hot apple cake.

Yield: 1/2 cup glaze

Don Farmer's Apple Cake Glaze

2 tablespoons butter
2 tablespoons packed brown sugar
2 tablespoons sugar
¼ teaspoon vanilla extract
2 tablespoons heavy cream

Combine butter, brown sugar, sugar, vanilla and cream in saucepan. Cook until mixture boils, stirring constantly. Boil for 1 minute. Pour over warm cake.

Yield: ½ cup glaze

The apple has long been associated with health, as Arabian tales speak of it as the healing fruit and the Norse gods ate an apple when they felt old age approaching. Even today we frequently hear the expression , "An apple a day keeps the doctor away."

Desserts

*F*rom apple pies, fried pies, apple dumplings and more, you won't believe the many tempting apple desserts available at the Apple Barn.

Brown Bag Apple Pie

¼ cup all-purpose flour
½ cup margarine
1 cup sugar
¼ cup all-purpose flour
½ cup sugar
¼ teaspoon cinnamon
8 apples, sliced
1 unbaked (9-inch) pie shell

Combine ¼ cup flour, margarine and 1 cup sugar in bowl and mix until paste is formed. Combine ¼ cup flour, ½ cup sugar and cinnamon in bowl and mix well. Toss apples in cinnamon mixture. Arrange apple slices in pie shell. Top with flour mixture. Place pie in brown paper bag and staple closed. Put bag on baking sheet and place on middle oven rack. Bake at 400 degrees for 1 hour. Remove pie from bag immediately. Return pie to oven to brown.

Editor's Note: Many of the brown bags in common use are made of recycled paper which may contain bits of metal and toxic materials. Avoid using those bags. The bottom of the bag may give recycling information.

Yield: 6 to 8 servings

Caramel-Apple Pie

2 unbaked deep-dish pie shells
1 (21-ounce) can Apple Barn™ apple
  pie filling
1 (14-ounce) bag caramel candies
1 (14-ounce) can sweetened
  condensed milk

Bake 1 pie shell at 350 degrees until light brown. Flatten remaining pie shell on waxed paper. Fill baked pie shell with apple pie filling. Cook caramels and condensed milk in top of double boiler until caramels are melted, stirring occasionally. Pour over pie. Top with remaining pastry, sealing edge and cutting vents. Bake at 350 degrees for 40 minutes or until golden brown.

Yield: 6 to 8 servings

Caramel Apple Cheese Pie

2 (3-ounce) packages cream cheese,
  softened
1/4 cup confectioners' sugar
1 (6-ounce) graham cracker piecrust
2 small Golden Delicious apples, peeled,
  sliced
2 tablespoons butter or margarine
1/4 teaspoon cinnamon
1/3 to 1/2 cup old-fashioned or reduced-
  fat caramel dip, heated

Beat cream cheese and confectioners' sugar in bowl until fluffy. Spread over bottom of piecrust. Sauté apples in butter in skillet for 5 minutes or until tender crisp. Drain apples on paper towels. Arrange apples on cream cheese. Sprinkle with cinnamon. Chill, covered, in refrigerator. Drizzle pie with dip.

Yield: 8 servings

Crumb-Top Apple Pie

½ cup margarine
½ cup firmly packed brown sugar
¾ cup sugar
1 tablespoon cornstarch
1 teaspoon cinnamon
1¼ cups all-purpose flour
6 large apples, sliced
1 unbaked pie shell

Cream margarine, brown sugar and sugar in mixer bowl until light and fluffy. Combine cornstarch, cinnamon and flour in bowl and mix well. Add creamed mixture to dry ingredients. Mix with fork until lumpy. Arrange apples in pie shell. Sprinkle topping over apples. Bake at 425 degrees for 10 to 15 minutes. Reduce heat to 350 degrees. Bake for 45 minutes or until apples are tender.

Yield: 6 to 8 servings

To make a braided piecrust edge, make pastry for a 2-crust pie and line the pie plate with half the pastry; trim the edge. Roll the remaining pastry into a 3x15-inch rectangle; cut lengthwise into 6 strips. Braid 3 strips. Add the remaining strips to the ends and continue to braid into a 30-inch braid. Moisten the edge of the pie shell with water. Place the braid on the rim and press gently into place.

Easy Apple Pie

4 to 5 cups sliced peeled apples
1 teaspoon cinnamon or allspice
5 slices bread, crusts removed
1½ cups sugar
1 egg
½ cup melted margarine

Arrange apples in 8x8-inch baking pan. Sprinkle with cinnamon. Cut each slice of bread into strips. Arrange bread strips over apples. Combine sugar, egg and margarine in bowl and mix well. Pour sugar mixture over bread. Bake at 350 degrees for 45 minutes.

Yield: 9 servings

Hester's Apple Pie

4 cups sliced peeled apples
¼ cup water
Cinnamon to taste
½ cup sugar
4 to 6 slices bread, crusts removed
½ cup melted margarine
1 cup sugar
1 tablespoon all-purpose flour
1 egg, beaten
1 teaspoon vanilla extract

Combine apples and water in casserole. Sprinkle cinnamon and ½ cup sugar on top of apples. Bake at 350 degrees for 15 minutes. Remove from oven. Cut each slice of bread into 6 strips. Arrange bread over apples. Combine margarine, 1 cup sugar, flour, egg and vanilla in bowl and mix well. Pour over bread strips. Bake at 350 degrees for 50 to 60 minutes or until golden brown.

Yield: 4 to 6 servings

Apple Kiwi Pie

Pie

1 cup sugar
2 tablespoons all-purpose flour
1/4 teaspoon salt
1/2 teaspoon apple pie spice
4 cups sliced peeled apples
1 cup sliced peeled kiwi
1 recipe Pastry
2 tablespoons margarine
1 egg white, beaten
1/2 cup confectioners' sugar
3 tablespoons maple syrup

Combine sugar, flour, salt and apple pie spice in bowl and mix well. Add apples and kiwi and toss gently to coat fruit. Spoon into prepared pie plate. Dot with margarine. Place remaining pastry over filling, fluting edges to seal. Cut several slits in pastry to vent. Brush with egg white. Bake at 400 degrees for 50 minutes or until golden brown. Combine confectioners' sugar and maple syrup in bowl. Drizzle over warm pie.

Pastry

1 cup all-purpose flour
1 cup oat bran
1 1/2 tablespoons sugar
1 teaspoon salt
3/4 cup shortening
1 egg, beaten
1/4 cup cold water
1 1/2 tablespoons vinegar

Combine flour, bran, sugar and salt in bowl and mix well. Cut in shortening until crumbly. Add egg, water and vinegar, mixing to form dough. Chill, wrapped in plastic wrap, until thoroughly chilled. Roll out half of pastry on lightly floured surface. Place in a 9-inch pie plate. Roll remaining pastry into circle and set aside.

Yield: 6 servings

Shredded Apple Pie

1½ cups sugar
¼ cup butter
2 eggs
½ teaspoon nutmeg
½ teaspoon cinnamon
2 cups shredded apples
1 unbaked (9-inch) pie shell

Cream sugar and butter in bowl until light and fluffy. Add eggs 1 at a time, mixing well after each addition. Add nutmeg, cinnamon and apples and mix well. Spoon apple mixture into pie shell. Bake at 350 degrees for 1 hour or until knife inserted in center comes out clean.

Yield: 6 to 8 servings

Swedish Apple Pie

2 or 3 medium Jonathan or Winesap
    apples, peeled, sliced
1 teaspoon cinnamon
1 tablespoon sugar
¾ cup melted butter or margarine
1 cup sugar
1 cup all-purpose flour
1 egg, beaten
½ cup chopped pecans

Fill pie plate ⅔ full with apples. Sprinkle with cinnamon and 1 tablespoon sugar. Combine butter, 1 cup sugar, flour, egg and pecans in bowl and mix well. Spread batter over apples. Bake at 350 degrees for 45 minutes or until golden brown.

Yield: 6 to 8 servings

Apple Dumplings

Dumplings

1¼ cups firmly packed brown sugar
⅓ cup butter, softened
½ teaspoon salt
1 teaspoon grated lemon peel
1 teaspoon cinnamon
8 medium apples, peeled, cored
Plain Pastry

Combine brown sugar, butter, salt, lemon peel and cinnamon in bowl and mix well. Fill each apple cavity with ⅛ of sugar mixture. Roll pastry into ⅛-inch thick rectangle on lightly floured surface. Cut into 8 squares. Place 1 apple in center of each square, bringing corners together at top. Moisten edges and pinch together. Place on baking sheet. Bake at 350 degrees for 30 minutes or until apples are tender.

Plain Pastry

2 cups sifted all-purpose flour
¾ teaspoon salt
⅔ cup shortening
4 to 6 tablespoons cold water

Sift flour and salt together in bowl. Cut in shortening. Add water 1 tablespoon at a time, mixing with fork until mixture forms ball.

Yield: 8 servings

Apple Dumplings with Cinnamon Syrup

Dumplings
1 cup sugar
1 teaspoon cinnamon
2 unbaked pie shells
8 apples, peeled, cored
2 tablespoons butter or margarine
Cinnamon Syrup

Combine sugar and cinnamon in bowl and mix well. Cut pie shells into 4 sections. Place 1 apple in center of each pastry section. Fill apple with cinnamon-sugar. Dot with butter. Fold pastry completely around apple. Repeat for each apple. Place apples in large baking dish. Pour syrup into bottom of dish. Bake at 450 degrees for 5 to 7 minutes. Reduce heat to 350 degrees. Bake for 30 minutes or until apples are tender.

Cinnamon Syrup
1 cup sugar
¼ teaspoon cinnamon
¼ cup butter or margarine
2 cups water

Combine sugar, cinnamon, margarine and water in saucepan. Cook until mixture boils, stirring constantly. Boil for 3 minutes.

Yield: 8 servings

Apple Pinwheel Dumplings

Pinwheels

1½ cup all-purpose flour
1 teaspoon salt
½ cup shortening
4 to 5 tablespoons cold water
4 cups shredded apples
½ teaspoon cinnamon
½ cup raisins (optional)
½ cup chopped pecans (optional)
1 recipe Syrup

Combine flour and salt in bowl and mix well. Cut in shortening until crumbly. Add water 1 tablespoon at a time, mixing with fork until mixture forms ball. Chill, wrapped in plastic wrap, for 2 hours. Roll pastry dough into long rectangle on lightly floured surface. Combine apples, cinnamon, raisins and pecans in bowl and mix well. Cover pastry with apple filling. Roll as for jelly roll, sealing edges. Slice into 1-inch slices. Arrange in 9x13-inch baking pan. Pour hot Syrup over pinwheels. Bake at 350 degrees for 45 minutes.

Syrup

2 cups water
½ cup margarine
1½ cups sugar
½ cup firmly packed brown sugar
½ teaspoon cinnamon

Combine water, margarine, sugar, brown sugar and cinnamon in saucepan. Cook until margarine has melted and sugar has dissolved, stirring constantly.

Yield: 8 to 12 servings

Easy Apple Dumplings

1 (8-ounce) can flaky refrigerated
  biscuits or crescent rolls
4 or 5 medium apples, peeled,
  quartered
½ cup melted butter or margarine
1 cup water
1 cup sugar
1 teaspoon cinnamon
Cinnamon-sugar to taste

Divide biscuits evenly among apple quarters. Wrap each apple quarter in dough. Arrange in greased 9x13-inch baking dish. Combine butter, water, sugar and cinnamon in bowl and mix well. Pour over apples. Sprinkle with cinnamon-sugar. Bake at 300 degrees for 40 minutes or until apples are tender.

Yield: 4 to 5 servings

The Romans preserved whole apples in jars of honey. These apples were served as a dessert to the elite.

118

Apple Crisp

4 cups chopped apples
½ cup water
3/4 cup all-purpose flour
1 cup sugar or firmly packed brown sugar
1 teaspoon cinnamon
2 tablespoons lemon juice
½ cup butter

Arrange apples in buttered 9x9-inch baking dish. Pour water over apples. Blend flour, sugar, cinnamon, lemon juice and butter in bowl until of consistency of granola. Sprinkle over apples. Bake at 350 degrees for 30 minutes or until crispy and golden brown.

Yield: 9 servings

Apple Crisp with Orange Juice

4 cups sliced peeled tart apples
¼ cup orange juice
1 cup sugar
¾ cup sifted all-purpose flour
½ teaspoon cinnamon
¼ teaspoon nutmeg
⅛ teaspoon salt
⅓ cup butter

Mound apples in buttered pie plate. Pour orange juice over apples. Combine sugar, flour, cinnamon, nutmeg and salt in bowl and mix well. Cut in butter until mixture is crumbly. Sprinkle sugar mixture over apples. Bake at 375 degrees for 45 minutes or until apples are tender and topping is crisp.

Yield: 6 to 8 servings

Apple Cheese Crisp

4 large apples, peeled, sliced
¹⁄₄ cup water
2 teaspoons lemon juice
³⁄₄ cup sugar
³⁄₄ teaspoon cinnamon
¹⁄₂ cup all-purpose flour
¹⁄₄ cup butter or margarine, softened
³⁄₄ cup grated Cheddar cheese

Arrange apples in greased 8x8-inch baking dish. Pour water and lemon juice over apples. Combine sugar, cinnamon, flour, butter and cheese in bowl until crumbly. Sprinkle over apples. Bake at 350 degrees for 30 minutes or until apples are tender.

Yield: 6 servings

Cheesy Apple Crisp

6 cups thinly sliced apples
³⁄₄ teaspoon cinnamon
³⁄₄ cup water
1¹⁄₂ cups sugar
1 cup all-purpose flour
¹⁄₄ teaspoon (or more) salt
¹⁄₂ cup butter or margarine
1¹⁄₂ cups shredded cheese

Arrange apples in shallow greased 9x13-inch baking pan. Sprinkle with cinnamon. Pour water over apples. Combine sugar, flour and salt in bowl and mix well. Cut in butter until crumbly. Stir in shredded cheese. Sprinkle cheese mixture over apples. Bake at 350 degrees for 30 minutes or until apples are tender and crust is brown and crisp.

Yield: 9 servings

Golden Delicious Apple Crisp

Apple Crisp

5 Golden Delicious apples, sliced
1 teaspoon lemon juice
1 teaspoon grated lemon peel
¼ teaspoon salt
1 teaspoon cinnamon
½ cup sugar
Crumb Topping

Combine apples, lemon juice, lemon peel, salt, cinnamon and sugar in bowl and mix until apples are coated. Spoon into greased 6-cup shallow baking dish. Cover with Crumb Topping. Bake at 350 degrees for 45 minutes.

Crumb Topping

½ cup sugar
½ cup all-purpose flour
½ cup butter
½ cup chopped nuts

Combine sugar, flour, butter and nuts in bowl and mix well.

Yield: 6 servings

121

Apple Cranberry Crisp

3 cups chopped apples
2 cups cranberries
1 cup sugar
½ cup water
½ cup melted butter
⅓ cup firmly packed brown sugar
¼ cup chopped pecans
1 to 1¼ cups rolled oats

Layer apples, cranberries, sugar and water in baking dish. Combine butter, brown sugar, pecans and enough oats to make mixture crumbly in bowl and mix well. Sprinkle over top of fruit. Bake at 350 degrees for 45 to 50 minutes or until apples are tender.

Yield: 6 to 8 servings

Peanut Butter Apple Crisp

4 cups sliced apples
¾ cup firmly packed brown sugar
½ cup all-purpose flour
½ cup quick-cooking oats
½ teaspoon cinnamon
½ teaspoon nutmeg
⅓ cup butter
1 cup peanut butter chips

Arrange apples in greased 9x9-inch baking dish. Combine brown sugar, flour, oats, cinnamon and nutmeg in bowl and mix well. Cut in butter until crumbly. Stir in peanut butter chips. Sprinkle over apples. Bake at 375 degrees for 30 minutes or until apples are tender.

Yield: 9 servings

Easy Apple Cobbler

5 Granny Smith apples, peeled, sliced
2 tablespoons water
1¼ teaspoons cinnamon
6 or 7 slices thin-sliced white bread, crusts removed
½ cup melted butter
1 egg, beaten
1¼ cups sugar

Pile apple slices in 7x11-inch or 8x8-inch baking dish. Sprinkle with water and cinnamon. Cut each slice of bread into 3 strips. Cover apples with enough bread strips to cover apples. Combine butter, egg and sugar in bowl and mix well. Spread butter mixture over bread. Bake at 350 degrees for 25 to 30 minutes or until rich golden brown.

Yield: 9 to 12 servings

Apple Ring

1½ cups all-purpose flour
½ teaspoon salt
½ cup shortening
4 to 5 tablespoons cold water
1 cup sugar
½ cup firmly packed brown sugar
½ cup margarine
2 cups water
4 cups shredded apples
Cinnamon to taste

Combine flour and salt in bowl. Cut in shortening until crumbly. Add water 1 tablespoon at a time, mixing with fork until mixture forms ball. Chill, wrapped in plastic wrap, for 30 minutes or longer. Combine sugar, brown sugar, margarine and water in bowl and mix well. Pour into 9x13-inch baking dish. Bake at 400 degrees until hot and bubbly. Reduce heat to 350 degrees. Roll chilled dough into rectangle on lightly floured surface. Sprinkle with apples. Roll as for jelly roll, sealing edges. Cut into 1½-inch slices. Arrange in hot syrup in baking dish. Sprinkle cinnamon over top. Bake at 350 degrees for 45 minutes or until golden brown.

Yield: 10 to 14 servings

Apple Roll

2 cups sugar
2 cups water
¼ teaspoon cinnamon
¼ teaspoon nutmeg
2 tablespoons butter
2 cups all-purpose flour
2 teaspoons baking powder
1 teaspoon salt
⅔ cup shortening
½ cup milk
2½ cups finely chopped apples
⅔ cup raisins

Combine sugar, water, cinnamon and nutmeg in saucepan. Cook until sugar dissolves, stirring occasionally. Stir in butter until melted. Set aside. Combine flour, baking powder and salt in bowl and mix well. Cut in shortening until mixture reaches fine crumb consistency. Add milk, stirring just until moistened. Knead on lightly floured surface 4 or 5 times. Roll into 9x12-inch rectangle. Sprinkle apples and raisins evenly over dough. Roll as for jelly roll, beginning with long side and sealing edges. Cut into 12 slices and arrange in greased 9x13-inch baking pan. Pour sugar syrup over slices. Bake at 375 degrees for 40 minutes or until golden brown.

Yield: 12 servings

Apple Kuchen

½ cup margarine
1 (2-layer) package yellow cake mix
½ cup coconut
1 (21-ounce) can Apple Barn™ apple
   pie filling
½ cup sugar
1 teaspoon cinnamon
1 cup sour cream
1 egg

Cut margarine into cake mix in bowl until crumbly. Stir in coconut. Pat mixture into lightly greased 9x13-inch baking pan, building up edges. Bake at 350 degrees for 10 minutes. Spread apple pie filling over top. Combine sugar and cinnamon in bowl and mix well. Sprinkle cinnamon-sugar over apples. Combine sour cream and egg in bowl and mix well. Drizzle sour cream mixture over apples. Bake at 350 degrees for 25 minutes or until light brown.

Yield: 15 servings

Make Apple Empañadas by filling flour tortillas with a mixture of 1 can apple pie filling, ¼ cup melted butter and 2 teaspoons cinnamon. Fold and secure with wooden picks. Deep-fry and sprinkle with cinnamon-sugar.

Sour Cream Apple Puff

2 tablespoons margarine
4 cups sliced peeled apples
$\frac{1}{2}$ cup sugar
2 tablespoons lemon juice
3 eggs, separated
$\frac{1}{2}$ cup sour cream
1 teaspoon grated lemon peel
1 teaspoon vanilla extract
$\frac{1}{4}$ cup sugar
$\frac{1}{4}$ cup confectioners' sugar

Melt margarine in 10-inch ovenproof skillet. Add apples, $\frac{1}{2}$ cup sugar and lemon juice. Cook, uncovered, for 10 minutes or until mixture is almost dry, stirring frequently. Remove $\frac{1}{2}$ of apples and set aside. Beat egg yolks in bowl. Add sour cream, lemon peel and vanilla and mix well. Beat egg whites in mixer bowl until soft peaks form. Add $\frac{1}{4}$ cup sugar gradually, beating until stiff peaks form. Fold egg yolk mixture into egg whites. Pour egg mixture over apples in skillet. Arrange remaining apples on top. Bake at 350 degrees for 25 minutes. Remove from oven and sift confectioners' sugar over top.

Yield: 6 to 8 servings

Baked Apple Pancake

4 large apples, peeled, sliced
1/2 cup butter or margarine
1 cup all-purpose flour
2 tablespoons butter or margarine
1/2 cup sugar
6 eggs
1 cup milk
Cinnamon-sugar to taste
Butter to taste

Sauté apples in 1/2 cup butter in skillet until apples are tender. Spoon apples into 9x13-inch baking pan. Combine flour, 2 tablespoons butter, sugar, eggs and milk in blender container and process until smooth. Pour over apples. Bake at 425 degrees for 15 to 20 minutes. Sprinkle with cinnamon-sugar and dot with butter. Bake for 5 minutes or until fluffy.

Yield: 15 servings

Apple Strudel

12 apples, chopped
1 cup chopped nuts
1 cup plain bread crumbs
2 cups sugar
2 sheets puff pastry

Combine apples, nuts, bread crumbs and sugar in bowl and mix well. Spread 1/4 of mixture down middle of each pastry sheet. Fold one side over filling. Top with 1/4 of filling. Fold remaining side over filling. Bake at 375 degrees until light brown.

Yield: 16 servings

Sally's Apple Tarts

¼ cup shortening
½ cup sugar
2 eggs
¼ teaspoon salt
¼ teaspoon baking soda
2¼ cups all-purpose flour
6 cups sweetened stewed apples
Confectioners' sugar to taste

Cream shortening and sugar in bowl until light and fluffy. Add eggs 1 at a time, mixing well after each addition. Add salt, baking soda and enough flour to make stiff dough. Roll dough on lightly floured surface. Cut 6 circles with round cookie cutter. Cut 6 circles slightly smaller for tops. Place larger rounds in bottom of muffin tin. Fill with apples. Place smaller circles on top. Bake at 350 degrees for 30 minutes or until tarts are light brown. Cool. Sprinkle generously with confectioners' sugar.

Yield: 6 tarts

Cinnamon Apple Wraps

1½ cups all-purpose flour
½ teaspoon salt
½ cup cold butter
4 to 5 tablespoons ice water
1 tablespoon butter, softened
2 large Golden Delicious apples,
    peeled, cut into 8 wedges each
¼ cup melted butter
⅓ cup sugar
1 teaspoon (or more) cinnamon
¾ cup apple cider

Combine flour and salt in bowl. Cut in ½ cup cold butter until crumbly. Add water 1 tablespoon at a time, mixing with fork until mixture forms ball. Chill, wrapped in plastic wrap, for 30 minutes or longer. Roll dough on lightly floured surface into 12-inch square. Spread with 1 tablespoon softened butter. Fold sides to center. Roll into 10x16-inch rectangle. Cut into sixteen 1x10-inch strips. Wrap 1 strip diagonally around each apple wedge. Arrange apple wedges, 8 per row, not touching, in a 9x13-inch baking pan. Brush with ¼ cup melted butter. Combine sugar and cinnamon in bowl and mix well. Sprinkle cinnamon-sugar over apples. Pour apple cider into baking pan. Bake on middle oven rack at 450 degrees for 20 to 25 minutes or until golden brown. Serve warm.

Yield: 16 apple wraps

Apple-Filled Oatmeal Cookies

1 cup chopped apples
1/4 cup raisins
1/4 cup chopped walnuts or pecans
1/2 cup sugar
2 tablespoons water
1 cup butter or margarine
1 cup firmly packed brown sugar
2 eggs
2 cups all-purpose flour
2 tablespoons baking powder
1/2 teaspoon salt
1 teaspoon cinnamon
1/2 teaspoon ground cloves
1/2 cup milk
2 cups rolled oats

Combine apples, raisins, walnuts, sugar and water in saucepan. Cook over low heat until thick and apples are tender, stirring frequently. Set aside. Cream butter and brown sugar in bowl until fluffy. Add eggs 1 at a time, mixing well after each addition. Add flour, baking powder, salt, cinnamon, cloves and milk and mix well. Stir in oats. Reserve 3/4 cup dough. Shape remaining dough into 1-inch balls. Place on lightly greased cookie sheet. Press thumb in center of each ball to make indentation. Spoon 1/4 teaspoon of apple filling into each indentation. Top with small amount of reserved dough. Bake at 375 degrees for 10 to 12 minutes.

Variation: May add 1 cup coconut at same time as oats.

Yield: 3 dozen cookies

Butterscotch Apple Cookies

2¹/₂ cups all-purpose flour
1 teaspoon baking soda
1 teaspoon cinnamon
1 teaspoon ground cloves
¹/₂ teaspoon nutmeg
¹/₂ teaspoon salt
1 cup firmly packed brown sugar
¹/₂ cup butter or margarine
1 egg
¹/₂ cup apple juice
³/₄ cup grated apple
¹/₂ cup chopped walnuts
2 cups butterscotch chips
2 tablespoons butter or margarine
¹/₄ teaspoon salt
1 cup confectioners' sugar
1¹/₂ tablespoons apple juice
Nuts (optional)

Combine flour, baking soda, cinnamon, cloves, nutmeg and ¹/₂ teaspoon salt in mixer bowl. Cream brown sugar and ¹/₂ cup butter in bowl until fluffy. Add egg and mix well. Add dry ingredients and ¹/₂ cup apple juice alternately, mixing well after each addition. Stir in apple, walnuts and 1¹/₂ cups of butterscotch chips. Drop by rounded teaspoonfuls onto greased cookie sheet. Bake at 350 degrees for 10 to 12 minutes. Combine remaining ¹/₂ cup butterscotch chips and 2 tablespoons butter in saucepan. Cook until butterscotch chips and butter are melted, stirring constantly. Add ¹/₄ teaspoon salt, confectioners' sugar and 1¹/₂ tablespoons apple juice, beating until of spreading consistency. Spread glaze over cooled cookies. Sprinkle with nuts.

Yield: 2¹/₂ dozen cookies

Apple Brownies

¾ cup melted margarine
1½ cups sugar
2 eggs
½ teaspoon salt
2 cups all-purpose flour
1 teaspoon baking soda
1 teaspoon baking powder
1 teaspoon cinnamon
2 cups chopped apples

Combine margarine, sugar, eggs and salt in bowl and mix well. Add flour, baking soda, baking powder and cinnamon and mix well. Stir in apples. Pour into ungreased 9x13-inch baking pan. Bake at 350 degrees for 30 to 40 minutes or until brownies pull away from side of pan.

Yield: 20 brownies

*Make Quick Apple Snacks by cutting a cored eating apple into ¼-inch slices.
Dip into lemon or pineapple juice and spread with peanut butter or dip slices of red-skinned
apples into lemon juice and sprinkle with curry powder or ground ginger.*

Nutty Apple Brownies

1 cup vegetable oil
2 eggs, beaten
1 teaspoon vanilla extract
2 cups self-rising flour
2 cups sugar
1 teaspoon cinnamon
1 teaspoon allspice
2 cups chopped apples
1/2 cup chopped nuts

Combine oil, eggs and vanilla in bowl and mix well. Add flour, sugar, cinnamon and allspice and mix well. Stir in apples and nuts. Pat into greased and floured 9x13-inch baking pan. Bake at 350 degrees for 45 minutes. Cool slightly before cutting into squares.

Yield: 20 brownies

Apple Oatmeal Bars

1 cup all-purpose flour
$\frac{1}{2}$ teaspoon salt
$\frac{1}{2}$ teaspoon baking soda
$\frac{1}{2}$ cup firmly packed brown sugar
1 cup quick-cooking oats
$\frac{1}{2}$ cup shortening
$2\frac{1}{2}$ cups thinly sliced apples
2 tablespoons butter
$\frac{1}{2}$ cup sugar

Sift flour, salt and baking soda together in bowl. Stir in brown sugar and oats. Cut in shortening until crumbly. Spread $\frac{1}{2}$ of oat mixture in greased 7x11-inch baking dish. Arrange apples over top. Dot with butter. Sprinkle with sugar. Cover with remaining oat mixture. Bake at 350 degrees for 40 to 50 minutes or until brown on top. Cut into bars.

Yield: 15 bars

Apple Squares

4 cups all-purpose flour
1 teaspoon salt
2 cups shortening
1 cup sour cream
6 large Golden Delicious apples, peeled,
 sliced
1 cup sugar
½ cup firmly packed brown sugar
1½ tablespoons lemon juice
¼ cup graham cracker crumbs
¼ cup fine dry bread crumbs

Combine flour and salt in bowl. Cut in shortening until crumbly. Stir in sour cream with fork until flour mixture is moistened. Chill, wrapped in plastic wrap, for 30 minutes or longer. Combine apples, sugar, brown sugar and lemon juice in bowl and mix well; set aside. Divide flour mixture in half. Roll 1 portion of dough into 10x15-inch rectangle on waxed paper. Place in 10x15-inch baking pan. Sprinkle with graham cracker crumbs and bread crumbs. Spread apple mixture over crumbs. Roll remaining flour mixture into 12x16-inch rectangle on waxed paper. Place over apple mixture. Fold edges over and crimp. Bake at 375 degrees for 1 hour. Cool on wire rack. Cut into squares.

Note: Flour mixture can be frozen for up to two months.

Yield: 3 dozen squares

Frosted Apple Squares

1 egg yolk
2/3 cup (about) milk
2 1/2 cups all-purpose flour
1 tablespoon sugar
1 teaspoon salt
1/2 cup shortening
1/2 cup margarine
6 to 8 apples, sliced
2 tablespoons all-purpose flour
1 1/2 cups sugar
1 teaspoon cinnamon
1 egg white
1 cup confectioners' sugar
3 tablespoons water
1 teaspoon vanilla extract

Beat egg yolk in 1 cup measure and add enough milk to make 2/3 cup. Combine 2 1/2 cups flour, 1 tablespoon sugar and salt in bowl and mix well. Cut in shortening and margarine until crumbly. Add egg yolk mixture and mix well. Roll half of dough on lightly floured surface into 12x15-inch rectangle. Place pastry in 12x15-inch baking pan. Arrange apples over pastry. Mix 2 tablespoons flour, 1 1/2 cups sugar and cinnamon in bowl and mix well. Sprinkle sugar mixture over apples. Roll remaining dough into 12x15-inch rectangle. Place on top of apples, sealing edges. Beat egg white until frothy. Brush on pastry. Bake at 350 degrees for 1 hour. Combine confectioners' sugar, water and vanilla in bowl and mix until smooth. Spread frosting over warm crust. Cut into squares.

Yield: 25 squares

Order Information

The Apple Barn Cider Mill & General Store
230 Apple Valley Road
Sevierville, Tennessee 37862
(800) 421-4606 or (423) 453-9319
Fax (423) 453-4060

Please send _____ copies of *The Apple Barn Cookbook Volume II* @ $15.98 each $ _____

Tennessee residents add sales tax @ $1.36 each $ _____

Postage and handling @ $3.00 each $ _____

Total $ _____

Name _____

Street Address _____

City _____ State _____ Zip _____

Telephone Number (   ) _____

[   ] Check enclosed made payable to The Apple Barn

[   ] VISA   [   ] MasterCard   [   ] Discover   [   ] American Express

Account Number _____ Expiration Date _____

Signature _____

[   ] **YES!** Please send me your latest Apple Barn Catalog. From homemade fruit butters to unusual novelty and gift items, you'll enjoy every page of the Apple Barn Cider Mill and General Store Catalog.

Photocopies will be accepted.